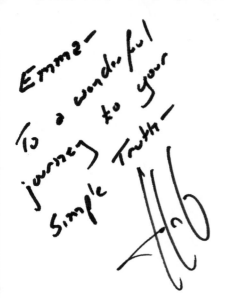

Emma—
To a wonderful
journey to your
Simple Truth—

The Simple Truth

The
Simple Truth

Meditation and Mindfulness for the Modern World

Jeff Cannon

W

Walton
Press

The author of this book does not dispense medical advice or prescribe the use of any technique as a form of treatment for physical, emotional, or medical problems without the advice of a physician either directly or indirectly. The intent of the author is only to offer information of a general nature to help you in your search for emotional and spiritual well being.

Simple Truth LLC
641 Avenue of the Americas, 3rd Floor
New York, NY 10011
info@simple-truth.com

Ordering Information:
Orders by U.S. bookstores and wholesalers please contact the publisher at the address above. Quantity special discounts are available on quantity purchases by corporations, associations, and others. For details, contact the publisher at the address above.

Printed in the United States of America

Publisher's Cataloging-in-Publication data
Cannon, Jeff.
The Simple Truth : Meditation and mindfulness for the modern world / Jeff Cannon

p. cm.
ISBN: 978-0-615-56268-1
Library/Academic ISBN: 978-1466497382

1. Meditation - mindfulness. 2. Self Help — stress management. 3. Self Realization. 4. Mind and Body. 5. Personal Transformation. I. Cannon, Jeff. II. Title.
HF0000.A0 A00 2011
299.000 00–dc22 2010999999
First Edition, November 2011
9 8 7 6 5 4 3 2

This book is dedicated to my family to whom I am eternally grateful: To my wife Laura, Weta and Walt and Jon and Marc and Pam and Mona and Brenna and Emily and Quinn and Kendall and Lily, and to my ever expanding family of people who I continue to meet and embrace every day.

Contents

Acknowledgements i

Introduction: Your Brain Can Change 1

My Simple Truth 5
- Your Old Programming in Action
- The Inevitable Question
- Your Programming
- Get Off Your Treadmill
- Don't Change, Evolve

Your Simple Truth 26
- Understand Your Operating System
- Meet the YOU Inside of You
- Four Steps to Your Personal Evolution

Step 1: Remove Your Outside Influences 41
- Silence Your Negative Inner Voice
- Increase Your Self-Awareness
- Overcome the Expectations of Others
- Be Comfortable With Your Faults
- Ignore the Influence of Consumerism
- Focus Your Unfocused Mind
- Exercise – Outside Message Awareness

Step 2: Build YOUR Foundation and Evolve 83
- Know Your State of Mind
- Learn to Breathe
- Develop Your Meditation Practice
- The Power of Meditation
- Meditation in Practice – Simple Repetition
- It Does Not Happen Overnight
- Types of Meditation
- Living Mindfully
- Live With CaRE
- Exercise – Playtime Meditation
- Exercise – Mindful Eating

Step 3: Find YOUR Simple Truth 124
- Find YOU inside of you
- YOU Are Your World
- Always Be Aware of Who YOU Are
- Be Comfortable in YOUR World
- Travel Your Path But Live In Your World
- Your Bags Are Already Packed
- Stay on Track to Your Simple Truth
- An Exercise – Follow Your Dreams
- An Exercise – Create a Visualization Collage

Step 4: Replace Your Old Programs 160
Peel Your Layers to Expose Your Core
Find Your Layers
Follow Your Triggers
Peel Back Your Layers
Replace Pain with Love
Forgive Yourself & Move On
See YOUR World
Pare Down Your Life to Your Simple Truth
Exercise – Redefine What You Have
Exercise – Find Your Triggers

Live with CaRE 200
Welcome to YOUR World
Make Good Choices with CaRE
Live YOUR Happiness Now
Enjoy Your Journey Warts & All
Your Simple Truth Is Your Compass
Take the Time to Appreciate Beauty & Art
Laugh at Your Mistakes and Evolve
Exercise – What Does YOUR CaRE Look Like?

Harmonize Your Life with Mindfulness 221
Love Your Social Net
There is No Work/Life Balance – Only Life
The Same But Different
Stop Swatting At Flies
Possess Nothing You Can't Afford To Lose
Daily Mindful Living
Minding Pain
Minding Fear
Exercise – Review Your Social Net

Tap into Life's Positive Energy 246
The Conservation of Energy
The Energy You Swim In
The Power of YES and NO
Train Yourself to Stay Open
Compassion & the Spirit of Yes
The Wisdom of Caution
Assert Your Positive Self
Create Your Own Vortex
Live Your Karma
Every Action

Constantly Evolve Your Simple Truth **268**
Challenge Your Automatic Pilot
Covet Your Time
Control Your Mobile
Enjoy Electronic Free Weekends
Dry, Dry, Drink
Most People Are Pretty Nice
Ask is Not a Four Letter Word
Ask Questions, Make No Judgments
Do Not Forget To Love
Commit 100%
Everything Is Not What You Want
What Will You Give Up

Acknowledgements

I would like to acknowledge all of those people without whom this book would not have been written. Most important to my wife Laura, without whose support and help this would never have gotten to print; Mary Wilberding who gave me my own Simple Truth with a push and a nudge to start this journey; Weta – for your constant reminder of what is important; Jan Pesce and Jason Wachob for your eyes, ears and insight; Dr. John Golfinos, Dr. Michael Margiotta, Jessica Schafrick and the rest of the NYU Medical team for the care you provided; Dr. Lawrence Lichenstein, Ph.D. for opening a door; Dr. Miles Neale PsyD, LMHC & Elena Brower for reminding me of the greater good we must constantly be aware of; Cyndi Lee and David Nichtern for enriching the world with a new generation of meditators; and to the yoga studios and teachers who continue to lead all those seeking to new heights.

Introduction:

Your Brain Can Change

Until just a few years ago almost everyone assumed that the brain didn't change. Many psychologists thought that the brain was set in its ways at a very young age; which meant that no matter what you did you could not change the way you think. You could only deal with your thoughts and habits through different forms of therapy.

Fortunately Buddhists and Eastern monks had different ideas as to how the mind worked. They realized that through meditation and mindful practices a person could attain a higher state of consciousness and reach a more peaceful and compassionate state of mind. They knew what Western scientists are just now finding out. That the brain can indeed change.

Doctors and scientists now refer to the physical element of this as neuroplasticity. That is, the ability of the brain to physically change in response to its environment. This ranges from cellular shifts that are involved in education, to cortical remapping, or restructuring in response to an injury. In both cases the brain is able to rewire its internal connections so that it can optimize how it functions.

In layman's terms the brain is able to change the way it is wired so that it can fit the way you live. It also means that it is possible for you to rewire your brain to fit they way you want to live, rather than having to live the way your brain was wired well before you were born.

To understand the reason this is so important we have to go back almost 140,000 years to the time when our ancestors first became what many scientists call early humans[1]. It took another 100,000 years for our ancestors to start displaying traits that we now consider as indicating modern humans. Even though exact dates are still bantered back and forth, and even with ongoing shifts in our humanity, most agree that we have remained hard wired for survival from our very first days on earth.

Our original genetic programming was a great feat. It enabled our ancestors to do more than just survive. It helped them rise to the top of the food chain, and then pushed them to change the world around them to suit their needs.

They did such a great job, they cultivated crops and mastered animals. They even created the 24/7 environment that you now live in. And therein lies the problem, your programming just wasn't built for the modern world we now call home. You are, in effect, trying to live in the 21st Century with a body that is still wired for a Paleolithic world.

If you think this is a lot to chew on, look at a real-world example. It can be found in a small, almond sized organ called the amygdala [ah-mig-dah-la]. This wonderfully small organ survived all of our evolutionary advancements. It can, in fact, be traced all the way back to our reptilian ancestors and is hard wired into the base of our brains in much the same way it still is

---

[1] By most accounts, Homo sapiens appeared about 140,000 years ago. Many archeologists and anthropologists contend that modern human behavior, the defining factor for modern humans, appeared roughly 40,000 years ago.

in theirs. No matter what we did to evolve and adapt, it didn't. In many ways it's a good thing it stayed around. Its purpose has always been to keep you safe and it is very good at what it does.

You see, when something happens that is out of the norm, the signals from the outside world are sent to your amygdala. It then sends out chemicals to your body that create feelings that range from discomfort and nervousness, to fear, anxiety, and even terror that you get from time to time.

You may recognize its work in the unease you get as you walk into a dark and creepy basement, or in that spinal shiver you feel when you see a spider. Yes, it still works just as it did 140,000 years ago. It still keeps you safe. But it has one problem. It doesn't realize that the 21st Century world you now live in simply does not have the same kind of threats that existed in the prehistoric world of your ancestors. It doesn't realize that when you are asked to give a speech you're really not in physical danger. It doesn't know that it's not helping your situation when it pumps you full of fear and anxiety.

Simple Truth

Just because you thought it, doesn't mean it's true.

It also doesn't know that the excitement elicited from an "ON SALE NOW" sign is not a life or death situation. All it knows to do is to send you into a fight or flight response, just as it has done for more than 140,000 years. But that doesn't mean you are stuck jumping every time it tells you to jump.

In fact, there is a pause button you can hit in the amygdala's programming that will allow you to choose how you respond and relate to the world around you. In doing so, you can start to make the kind of life choices you need to in order to live the life you love, and not the one your old programming is forcing you to live.

It doesn't stop there. The same programming that was hardwired into your ancestors also controls your life in other ways. When you feel frustrated, confused or out of place because of the way the world works, it is not because of you. It is your internal programming.

You see, with all of our progress we changed the world around us, but we never bothered to update our own operating system. We simply didn't know how, until now.

Now you can change your programming by learning to use the basic practices of meditation and incorporating mindfulness into your life. You can also learn to expand on them with a process I call Living with CaRE. It will enable you to evolve the way you respond to the world around you. It will help you evolve on a personal level. Not by growing an extra finger or waking up to find you have a tail, but by updating your software. By rebooting your system so that it works for the modern world you now live in rather than for the world our ancestors inhabited.

What took me twenty years of meditation to learn, ten hours of brain surgery to see, and four months of recovery to realize is all here. It is the path to your personal evolution through your own Simple Truth.

My Simple Truth

Before 2009 I was a driven entrepreneur who fared far better running my own business than working in the corporate world. I started my career at the world's largest public relations firm, Burson Marsteller. It was a great introduction to the machinations of Madison Avenue and the business of public relations. But two years into it I knew it wasn't the right fit. I wanted something more creative, something that allowed me to be me.

So I packed up and followed several friends out to Los Angeles in search of a new adventure in the film industry. In time I produced a number of projects. I was on the right path, I just couldn't deal with the politics. I realized while I loved the work, the politics were just something I would never be suited for. So, six years after arriving in L.A., I sold the production company I had started to a West Coast ad agency and returned to the world of Madison Avenue – albeit in a West coast kind of way. It worked for a while. Until that is, a funny thing called the Internet appeared, and once again I sprinted in search of new opportunities.

I was part of the original team behind the Los Angeles Times' first website in 1996. I wrote two books for McGraw Hill. I got married and returned to New York where I ran a major digital agency for three years. I even started my own agency when I couldn't take the corporate world any more. I even grew it into a seven figure firm with a healthy roster of clients.

But all of this came to an end when I got the news that rocked my life. Doctors told me that I had, not one, but seven brain tumors in 2009. It literally stopped me in my tracks. It slammed shut a major door on my life. But at the same time it opened up a much larger one that I had ignored for a long, long time. It was my own first introduction to my own Simple Truth.

When I look back I realize there were plenty of signposts that would have gotten me to where I now am quicker. I should have paid attention to them, but I was just running too fast to recognize them. There was no course in college for this. There was no roadmap or roadside rest stop for directions. There was just the University of Hard Knocks and the School of Life.

It took a ten hour brain surgery and several months of recovery for me to put it all together. But once I was shown how the human brain works up close and personally I began to understand how connected we all are in ways most of us can't even begin to fathom.

So how did I get here? Looking back I realize the cascade of events started well before that day in my doctor's office. It started in 2003. At that time I had left a job running a top digital ad agency to go out on my own and start my own firm. I had a not so crazy idea that if I was so unhappy with my current job I could go on my own and create the life I was looking for by creating the job I loved.

I started with a dynamic office environment. I hired young people and gave them the freedom every young person wants to show what they can do. I helped to guide and mentor their efforts in a productive way.

At first it went great. I grew the business. I added clients. I added staff. I got written up in PRWeek. But somewhere along the way things started going wrong. Clients started asking for more, which should have been great. But the staff was too young to understand that with freedom comes responsibility. Balls were dropped. Clients became unhappy. So I had to jump in and attend to more and more of the details myself.

I started working sixty and seventy hour weeks. The 24/7 atmosphere, that at first generated dynamic ideas, quickly turned into a center of stress. It wore on me and everyone else. But I thought that's just what entrepreneurs did. They stressed.

I thought of the work as a gamble. "If I can only push it for a little while longer I can jump the entire group to the next level and then I'll be fine." I'm not the only entrepreneur to have rolled the dice like that.

I pushed harder. I assumed that if I pushed harder, I would get us over the hump and to where I wanted to go. Only the harder I pushed, the more I seemed to backtrack. I started taking on clients and projects I didn't really want to in order to pay the salaries I needed to grow the agency. In just a few years after its launch, it was no longer the agency I wanted to run. Somewhere along the way my agency had turned into exactly the kind of agency I left.

It had become about numbers not creativity. It valued billable hours and profits over thinking and creativity. But that never occurred to me at the time. I was pushing too fast to see what was going on. I was running on my own treadmill, trying to build a larger agency for the sake of being larger, for the right to brag about my annual billings instead of creating something that I really wanted to create.

Then, in 2008 two things happened. First, the economy softened and clients began to cut budgets. I worked harder. Not better, but harder. At the same time, my father's fight with cancer took a steep slide for the worse. He went from being a dynamic physical force in my life, to a dynamic spiritual one. He remains to this day a reminder of what real dignity and strength is all about. His relationship with my mother also taught me a great deal about the larger world of spirituality that surrounds all of us.

I tried to see him as much as possible, but with my business getting bumpy I saw everything I was doing as a trade-off. At the end of 2008, just several weeks after my last visit with him, my father passed on. And I say "passed on" for a reason. I attended the funeral, after which I did what I thought I was supposed to do. I returned to New York City, kept a stiff upper lip and tried my best to carry on.

It worked for a while, but only on the outside. Inside I was a mess. Several months later when the economy went into free-fall in 2009, it took my business with it. Clients slashed budgets left and right and the young team I built just could not carry the load. It was the straw that broke the camel's back. The gamble that worked in an up economy was failing in the now down one. I spent the better part of 2009 whittling away at my team in layoff after layoff.

But at that point my heart was just no longer into it. I thought it was the worst year of my life. Was, that is, until the day I found myself sitting beside my wife learning about the need for an immediate operation – brain surgery.

When I looked around my office the next day I truly saw what I had created. I also realized what I missed in doing so. What I created was now a mess. It was still making money, but it was a far cry from what I had set out to do. Even worse, what I had missed was unforgivable.

I dealt with the news of my tumors by ignoring the reality of it. I started to think about my timeline and how quickly I could get back to work to make everything right. My doctor just shook his head. He told me it would be three months at best before I could even think about getting out of the house. It would more likely be six months or a year before I could go back to work.

That was when it really struck me that there was no way my business could survive that long without me. And I would not survive if I tried to keep it alive. Apparently the powers that be knew just one life-changing event was not enough to make me see the realities of the world, the larger world, that we live in. Apparently I needed a whole bunch of them. There was little left to do but close everything down and take a break from it all.

Four intense weeks later I turned out the lights, locked the door for the last time and tossed the keys through the mail slot. I walked down the street and into the first barber shop I could find. "Shave it all off," I said. They looked at me and laughed. Who knows, maybe they thought I had enlisted and was trying to beat the military's barber to the job. When they found out what I was doing, they would not let me pay them. They would not even let me leave a tip. Instead they gave me a lock of my hair from the floor.

The surgery itself lasted for more than ten hours. When I woke up the first thing I said to the doctor was "tell my wife I need more cowbell." To this day I am not sure why I picked this line. But somehow my brain fell on a favorite skit from a classic Saturday Night Live show. It was something that my wife and I had watched just before the surgery; a skit where Christopher Walken plays a music mogul, asking for more of the wrong thing. It was as if my brain picked the first file it could find that had a relevant message. It was also a hysterical skit; as if something inside was trying to say, "We've got a couple of glitches in here, but I'm okay." It was the start of my realization that there was more going on inside my brain, and my whole body, than I had anticipated. It was as if I was not running the show, but just along for the ride.

The first few nights of my recovery I had no dreams. When I closed my eyes I saw nothing. I only saw a textured surface – like an extremely close-up photo of black and white sand. Nothing moved and nothing changed. It was static. Then four days later I began to see some color in the photo; not much, just a shade of mauve or light brown. Several days later I closed my eyes and I remember the sand started to move in a long, slow rhythm. For the first time I realized that my brain was re-booting itself. Just like a computer, only slower.

After I was released from the hospital and sent home to recover I continued to watch as my brain reconnected. I remember waking up one morning to the smell of coffee. It did not even occur to me that I had not been able to smell for several weeks. But once it was back, my sense was so acute that I could pick up details and nuances that I was never able to in the past. I realized my brain was rebooting my senses as if I were connecting a printer or a scanner or some other peripheral to a computer. The sense of taste came later, only more acute than I had ever had it. Finally, one morning I woke up remembering my dream from the night before. It was a vivid dream of sailing and exploration; of floating on the sea. Almost like a lucid dream where I was partially awake, observing the action from my mind's eye.

That was it. It was close to three weeks after my operation, and I was up and running. Well, at least my wiring was.

My body continued to recover, but I was floored at how my brain had re-booted itself. It truly was just like watching a computer. While my body continued to recover I began to explore more and more about what I had witnessed

I have always had a fascination with the human mind. But I wanted to learn more about neural networks, integral health and neuroplasticity. I spoke to Western doctors and Eastern yogis. I listened to lectures. I even met a man who had recovered from Bell's palsy, who told me how his sense of taste recovered in stages – first bitter, then sour, then salty and finally sweet. I spoke to a friend who had battled alcoholism and had similar experiences during his recovery. I read up on the brain, on the value of meditation to both Buddhists and to CEOs. I also learned about recovery for addictions, eating disorders and other afflictions.

What I learned was this. When we created the computer we created it in our own image. Without thinking we based it on the only processor we were familiar with – our own brain. While the systems we created are not as powerful, nor as elegant as our own internal computer, the basic architecture is quite similar. To me if it could be rebooted then it could be reprogrammed; and I am not alone in that thinking.

That is the idea behind this book. To give you a way to reprogram your wiring and your life based on your own Simple Truth, rather than the needs, whims and desires of the world around you. Simply put, there is a way to turn your Life into a life you enjoy, rather than a life you dread. Yours truly can be a life you would love to live if you can live by your own Simple Truth.

Your Old Programming in Action

Unlike a computer, your internal programming does not issue command prompts or error messages. It doesn't send you an email or an instant message. It communicates through the habits, fears and spontaneous reactions you have to the world around you. It is a wordless system that speaks through your emotions. That is the way your old programming communicates with you.

Your amygdala speaks to you through the fear, discomfort and nervousness that you feel. The rest of your programming does the same thing when it directs you to act without thinking, jump to an answer too quickly, or acquiesce to someone else's whims even as you wonder why you're not sticking up for yourself.

In looking back at my life before the surgery I realize three things. First, all of those job changes and moves were the result of an unhappiness I had with the way my life was going at the time. Almost as if some ancient impulse was saying, "this hunting ground is no longer any good. You need to move." I used my dissatisfaction with my job as the rationale for my moves. But in reality it was my entire life that was going in the wrong direction. I just didn't know it.

On the surface I thought everything was fine. That this was the way life was. I had no idea how wrong I was. So every time I moved I thought I was making things better. When in reality, deep down inside, the real ME was trying to tell me that my life choices were heading me in the wrong direction.

Over the centuries different cultures have referred to this when they speak of the Dharma. Krishna refers to this concept in the ancient text of the Bhagavad Gita when he tells a soldier, "Better your own dharma badly performed than the dharma of another done perfectly." Taken literally, Krishna is telling this warrior is that it is better to follow his true calling, even if it means killing others, than to try and be something he is not. It was written on the portals of the ancient Greek temple of Delphi thousands of years ago "Know thyself." Shakespeare had the same idea in Hamlet when Polonius said, "to thine own self be true." It is a universal idea that has been around since the beginning of time. It is not owned by any one sect, or religion. It is free for anyone to learn from and incorporate into their life.

I call it living by your Simple Truth. Your Simple Truth is there whether you listen to it or not. But if you don't listen to it, you will never be able to find the happiness you want nor live the life you love.

This concept should not be a surprise to anyone. You know deep down inside what is right for you. You know when you're going off track. Your body doesn't know how to tell you this in plain English. But it does send you messages using the only way it has. It speaks through the impulses that you act on, the emotions you display, and the actions you take without knowing why.

Often we mistranslate those messages into "I need to find a new job" or "I should move to a new city," or "I need to find a new boyfriend or girlfriend," or "I need another drink." Unfortunately, none of those answers will get you to where you truly want to go. They simply put you into a place where your actions rarely end up being in your best interest.

My second realization was that throughout my life I have always had a natural inclination toward a more balanced lifestyle and toward meditative practices. I just never had the self-confidence to commit to them fully. I dabbled in them and always relegated my own well being to a level of lesser importance – somewhere on par with the time I allotted to the gym. I never allowed it to be a priority in my life. It was simply something I was mindful of, but nothing that I would ever allow to overshadow my "career."

Instead of pursuing what was right for me I succumbed to the whims and pressures of those around me, to some imaginary timeline society put in front of me. In the end, I succeeded in creating a life that was counter to my own Simple Truth, and not one I wanted to live.

Throughout my life I have been given opportunities, signs if you will, to pursue a life I would have loved. While I may have explored them on the surface, I never really paid attention to them. Instead I kept on a safe track – on my treadmill. It was as if something was trying to nudge me in the right direction, but I just refused to listen.

This first of these signs showed itself just after I graduated high school. I started to practice martial arts. I was quickly drawn, not to the sparring, but to the meditative quality of the more formal practices I seemed to gravitate toward.

After college I sought out a Grand Master by the name of Mr. Nakamura. He was a man renowned in the Japanese martial art known as Seido. He ran a very traditional school where meditation played a primary role in his teachings. The practice appealed to me so much that I thought about leaving the corporate world I was in to focus on martial arts. Instead, I quit my job, moved to Los Angeles and joined the film industry. I obviously wanted a change, but I just couldn't pull away from the idea of a career. For me, the idea of making films kept me from pursuing what I realize now could have been a wonderful path to pursue.

Once in Los Angeles I gravitated toward Eastern philosophies and mindfulness practices. I sought out another leader in the martial arts, Grand Master Bong Soo Han. He is credited with bringing the Korean practice of Hapkido to the United States. Once again, I balanced my life with one foot in the business world and one foot dedicated to the martial arts. Once again, I still did not have the self-confidence to leap off of the treadmill I was on and pursue a life that followed my natural inclination toward meditation and mindfulness.

At about this time I learned some startling news. Doctors found that I had what was called an acoustic neuroma – a benign tumor that would leave me deaf in my right ear. It was the first sign that I had what is called neurofibromatosis. Normally this is a hereditary disorder, passed down from generation to generation. But mine was a random genetic mutation that predisposed me to tumors in my brain and spine.

We all have our weaknesses and this was to be mine. As one doctor at the time told me, there was no rhyme or reason to it. I was just dealt a bad hand of cards. What started as a simple decision to lose my hearing in order to save my life would end up being the first of, to date, six brain surgeries over a span of almost twenty years. Each one associated with a time of heightened stress in my life. It was as if something was trying to send me a signal – stress is killing you. It was one that I was too obstinate to see.

It wasn't until the last surgery that I really connected the two things – stress and my body's predilection toward tumors. When I went into prolonged periods of high stress my body simply did not have the energy to keep the tumors at bay. We all have natural weaknesses in our bodies. It's one of the Simple Truths everyone must live with. Mine just came through a little bit louder and clearer than most. If only I had listened to it earlier.

So for the past twenty years I ignored the reality of my Simple Truth. Instead I stopped my life every few years to undergo another brain surgery. When I recovered, I would jump back into work and push harder in my pursuit of more money and better titles. Part of it was my effort to prove that I was in control and that I was not going to let this disorder control my life. If anything my effort to take control gave me just the opposite. Talk about just not listening to the signs.

My final realization was that my most recent surgery was not the result of a single event. Yes the global economic meltdown was a factor in my business's collapse, but that was not why I was where I was. My predicament was the result of a lot of little choices that I had made throughout the years that put me in a position where I was forced to make a no-win decision. Due to a myriad of smaller, seemingly insignificant choices, I had created a life that simply went against my own unique Simple Truth.

No one choice would have led me down a different path. But had I been more aware of where my life was going, had I made several choices differently, I could have guided my life in any direction I wanted to take it. I could have stopped pushing so hard. I could have taken better care of myself. I could have...but I didn't. All those little choices I made along the way put me in the position where I was forced to make a big decision about my surgery and my life.

What I realized was that our lives are not dictated by the big decisions we agonize over, but by the smaller choices we make without even thinking about them. If we can change the way we make the smaller choices in our lives, then we can truly guide our lives in any direction we want to go. Coupled with the knowledge of how our old programming works, it became clear to me that every one of us could create a paradigm shift in our lives and live the lives we want more easily than I ever thought possible.

Confirmation that my ideas weren't crazy came almost a year after my surgery. At that time I returned for what we all thought would be another pre-surgery planning meeting to remove a tumor my doctor was forced to leave behind due to the risk involved with removing it earlier.

In the eighteen months that followed my surgery I had changed my diet, I had returned to a practice of yoga and morning meditation. I had changed the little choices I made every day about how to live my life. In the end, my surgeon was amazed by what he saw. My seventh tumor had stopped growing. Even with my predilection to them, something had shifted. In the end he shrugged and said, "If it's not growing there's no reason to go in." He smiled and gave me a smirk when he said "keep doing whatever it is you're doing. It seems to be working."

It was like waking from a dream. I realized that our lives truly are precious gifts that can be taken away in a moment if we allow them to. I also realized that a series of bad choices, no matter how small they are, can accumulate into a long, slow, painful spiral of misery. I was fortunate that my spiral was stopped by my brain tumors. I am also extremely grateful that I have found a way to change the lives each of us lives.

There are still tumors inside of me. They are part of my own Simple Truth. Whether they grow or not is entirely up to me. They are a constant reminder of how important it is to live the life that I want to live. They are also a constant reminder that it is never too late to change your life into the one you were born to live.

The Inevitable Question

No matter what you do, at some point in your life you will ask yourself a very simple question: "is this all there is?" It may not come out in so many words, but the thought will be there.

It might be a question about living up to your potential, or if you are going to achieve everything you are capable of. You might look back to see if you have checked off all the boxes and filled in all the buckets you created so many years ago. You might start second guessing choices you made, or even go so far as to pick out a few moments from your life and wonder where you would be if you had made different decisions. Some of you may even think about the things you did and wonder whether the joys of accomplishment justified the costs the inflicted.

Unfortunately no matter what you achieved your answer will most likely be the same; that wherever you ended up is not quite where you intended to be, or that the life you now have is just not quite what you had planned.

You shouldn't be surprised that you feel like this. It is something everyone goes through. You are not feeling this way because you haven't succeeded. You are feeling this way because you are human, and self-doubt is part of human nature. Self doubt helps to keep you with the rest of the tribe. It causes you to doubt the direction you want to go is the right way just because nobody else is going there. Again, that kept our ancestors alive 40,000 years ago. But today, it's just not as necessary in the world we now live in.

In the end, it is in our nature to be social creatures. It is a survival trait. We are hard wired to be this way. Our very desire to be together, to work together, to cooperate is one of our greatest evolutionary advantages we have. But it can also work against us. We end up worrying about where we are in the pecking order and where we are in the social ranks. We worry about whether or not we measure up.

Just as your programming directs you to act through the habits you have formed, your true self, the real YOU, speaks to you through self questioning like this. It urges you to try something new or different. It pushes you to seek answers to your own questions. Had I realized my urge to change careers and move to new places was really a cry to change my life, I would have done so decades ago. But I didn't.

Simple Truth

Self doubt is the emotion your old programming creates when you question it mid -action.

The good news is that it is never too late to change. You can override your programming whenever you want. You can influence your life so that you can live the way you want to, regardless of what others say. It just takes determination to do so.

So after you are done beating yourself up about what could have, would have, and should have been, start looking ahead at what will be. Ask yourself "If I'm not happy with what I have, then what do I truly want?" The answer to this lies in your own Simple Truth, and it may surprise you.

You see, no matter how dire your circumstances, no matter how little you think you may have achieved or how much more you have yet to do in your life, always remember that this is YOUR life. You have far greater control over it than you think. You simply have to override 140,000 years of programming to do so. Even though you have become very comfortable with your old programming, breaking through it is not as hard as you might think.

Your Programming

Picture your ancestors 40,000 years ago. They had no claws to hunt with. They had not scaled plating for protection. All they had was human nature to help them fight their way out of the forests. Their intelligence helped them create tools. Their bodies helped them wield them. But it was their human nature that truly set them apart.

It was their need to band together and form tribes that kept them ahead of the other animals. It was their need to socialize that drove them to build huts, houses, towns and cities. Their basic programming drove them to domesticate animals, till the soil and change the environment to suit their needs – for better and for worse.

That same human nature still drives you in everything you do. Your impulse to bond and please others causes you to make decisions that may not be in your best interest. The fight or flight response that enabled your ancestors to stay alive now leads you to make hasty decisions that rarely lead to living the life you actually want to live. And yes, the self-questioning that once caused your ancestors to think of new ways to do things has now turned inward to fill you with self-criticism and doubt. It is also being leveraged by advertisers, political candidates and companies of all kinds to sell you what they want you to buy.

If you're wondering what your programming sounds like, you simply have to listen to that inner voice when it counts out everything that you have done wrong or have left undone at the end of your day. It rises up as self-criticism every time you look in the mirror hoping for perfection, only to see the lines and wrinkles that make you think less of yourself. It comes alive when someone makes you feel so bad that you want to change the very clothes you wear.

With all of our technological advances we now have, most of us still have not learned how to manage our own inner voices. We still let it rule our lives even when we know better, because that is how we are wired. It is why most of us have never learned how to simply be happy, because as a species we are wired to get along, not to find our own happiness. We are wired for survival, not to pursue our own Simple Truth.

The good news is we are far enough along on our evolutionary track that you can change this. You now have the tools that will enable you to interrupt that old programming so that you can quiet your inner voice and enjoy the world around you. You can hit the pause button in your programming so that you can enjoy your life. I know, because I did it myself.

Simple Truth

For the first time you have the tools you need to change your relationship with the world around you. They are yours. Pick them up and use them.

The science, the practice, the lessons I learned during my recovery gave me the material to find my own pause button and to write this book. There is no mystery to what I am telling you. We have simply reached a time in human evolution where we finally have the wherewithal to take everything we have learned to the next level. It is why I don't call this kind of transformation change, I call it personal evolution.

What follows are basic methods that monks and doctors, universities and temples around the world have proven to work. They will provide you with tools you can use to shift the way you respond to the world around you in order to live with a greater level of awareness, with less stress, and the power to live the life you love. The Simple Truth will enable you to evolve into a happier and more fulfilled person than you have ever been. It has for me.

So if you want to gain control of your life. If you want to get off your treadmill so that your life is truly YOURS, then read on and start living your own Simple Truth.

Get Off Your Treadmill

I know every day is different. But help me out. Does this in some way represent your day?

> You wake up, drink a cup of coffee, go to work and deal with whatever the day throws at you. After you shut down your computer and leave your work you go home and have dinner. Perhaps you watch some television before getting ready for bed. Perhaps you read a book or have a drink or two. You wonder why you don't have more time in your life to enjoy it. Perhaps you look at your social calendar and wonder why it is not what it should be. Perhaps it's filled with people you only connect with superficially, or not at all. You shrug. Once tucked into bed you toss and turn before you finally drift off to sleep only to wake up to do it all over again.

Is that close? Maybe one day you break your pattern by treating yourself to a new outfit on your way home. Or maybe you pick up a larger flat screen high definition television set. But no matter what you buy soon after you get it home the feeling of accomplishment starts to fade and you begin to look for the next little purchase that you hope will give your life the satisfaction you deserve.

If this is you then you are on the proverbial treadmill of life running a nine-minute mile. It's not fast enough for the

Olympics but it is enough to raise a sweat. It's faster than a comfortable walk so you have to focus on where your feet are landing, rather than enjoy the view. All you can really think about is where your foot will land next so you don't trip and fall.

Just like running on a treadmill the pattern of your life will not change unless you reach out and reset the mechanisms that control your life. In the end no matter how many dinners you enjoy, no matter how many outfits you own, no matter how large your home is, none of it will ever be enough to quiet that voice in your head asking "Is this all there is?" It never will.

The reason for this is simple. The habits you are comfortable with, the rules you live by and the desires you chase after are all guided by your old programming. The same programming that was hard wired into your genes thousands of years ago.

> ***Simple Truth***
>
> *Don't' be afraid of going too slowly. Just don't stand still.*

Well, now it's time to evolve. Not by growing another finger or a longer neck, but by changing the way you interact with the world around you. By learning how to pause your programming and modify the way you live your life.

You have the freedom to choose what you do. You have the power to change the pace of your treadmill or turn it off altogether. It's up to you to do so.

Don't Change, Evolve

Stepping off the treadmill is one of the hardest things to do in life. But it's far from impossible. Just by acknowledging that treadmill even exists, means you're already halfway there. If you can recognize that something in your life is not working right, even if you don't know what it is, you are already on the path to your own personal evolution.

The next step is to understand that YOU do not need to change. YOU are fine just the way you are. What needs to change is the path you are on. What needs to change is the way you respond and interact with the world around you. You need to evolve beyond your present life, so that you can become a more aware person and a better you.

For most of my existence I wasn't aware that anything was wrong with my life. I just had a feeling that things weren't quite as they should be. All through my life, I've had great jobs and a solid career. I have met amazing people. I met and married a woman I love. I enjoyed myself immensely. But throughout all of this, my life just wasn't all that I thought it should be or could be. No matter what I had, I felt unsatisfied and kept searching for more. I was frustrated because I knew that the life I wanted was out there. I just wasn't sure where.

The reason for that is simple. I either kept trying to change who I was to fit someone else's ideals, or I tried to change the world I was living in. I did what we all do. I listened to my old programming. I did what humans have done for centuries – I searched for happiness by trial and error. I moved to new cities, I changed jobs; I even broke up with whomever I was dating. I did all of this in an effort to get to where I thought I wanted to go. But no matter how much I tried to change my world, inside I was still ME. Even if I didn't know it, I still had my own Simple Truth. And without understanding my own Simple Truth, no matter what I did, I always ended up in the same place.

I imagine the same is probably true for you. No matter what you try to change in your world, sooner or later the world you create ends up disappointing you. The problem is that no matter where you go or how you change your world, you will always be

YOU. And YOU are not the problem. Your programming is. Your programming prevents the outer you that everyone knows, from following YOUR path, the path you were born to pursue.

At your core YOU do not need to change. You simply need to learn how to turn off the old programming that prevents you from living YOUR life the way you were meant to. This is what finding and living by your own Simple Truth is all about. Finding your own Simple Truth so you can live the life you love.

Only by doing this can you find the real happiness and success you deserve no matter what this crazy world throws in your direction.

Your Simple Truth

There are many truths in your life. There are universal truths (like the force of gravity). There are human truths (the fact that we must eat in order to stay alive). And there are personal truths (those that define who you are as a person and as a spirit). Whether you acknowledge any of these does not matter. The fact is they still exist.

Ignoring gravity will not make it any easier to fly. Ignoring the need for food will not make it any easier to live without it. Ignoring your own simple truths will not make finding happiness any easier. Those truths will still be there. They will still define who you are and how to best live your life. Ignoring them will simply make your existence a life of trial and ERROR – with the word "error" in capital letters.

Learning about your own Simple Truth will give you the guidelines that will help you live your life the way YOU were meant to live it. It will help you get where you need to go quicker and with fewer missteps.

To live by your own Simple Truth simply means to act in accordance with who YOU are and to follow YOUR own path wherever it leads. It does not mean doing whatever you want no matter what the consequences may be. It means living with compassion and respect for others. It means living in mindful harmony with those around you. This, as you will find later on, is a part of living your Simple Truth.

Buddhism refers to this path as the dhamma-vinaya - or literally the "path of discipline." The discipline involves training yourself to have a greater awareness of yourself and the world around you. It involves being aware of the impact the everyday choices you make will have; so that you can make the kind of choices that will keep you on your path no matter where it takes you.

Simple Truth

Life is not made or lost through earth shattering decisions, but in the little choices you make every day.
Make good choices and your life will move in the right direction all by itself.

Because everyone has their own Simple Truth, or their own dharma, everyone will have a slightly different path to take. There is no wrong path. There are no better paths. There is only your path to which you must stay true.

Your path will also not stay the same. It will evolve as you grow and evolve. Every choice you make and experience you explore along the way will modify your life. Each will present a new opportunity for you to refresh your life and to grow closer to your own Simple Truth, or to move you further away from it. No matter what the choice is, no matter how large or how small it seems, everything that you do will modify your life to some degree. This is why it is important for you to learn how to make the kind of little choices that will move your life in the direction YOU want to go.

During my recovery I had time to reflect on my life. I couldn't help but think about the choices I made. I was stunned by the opportunities that had been presented to me throughout my life. I still wonder what would have happened had I pursued those that I ignored, or chose not to take some that I followed. The only answer I can give is that they probably would have led me to the exact place where I am now. I may just have gotten here a bit quicker.

Most of you have probably experienced something similar in your lives. When presented with opportunities, rather than go off on your own, you kept to the path that everyone told you to follow. You pursued their ideas rather than your own, trusting them to know better. But even if the people you relied on had more experience than you, they more than likely guided you on their path, rather than yours. So the voice of your programming told you to stay their course and kept you running on your treadmill, never once allowing you to consider that it was leading in a direction you may not have wanted to go.

When I had a moment of clarity and became aware of how our programming works to keep us in line I got angry. I thought, "Why didn't anybody ever tell me about this? Why didn't anyone tell me what to look for?" But then I realized, up until recently, we simply didn't know. We weren't at the point that we are right now, where science is now proving what Eastern practices have known for centuries.

I also realized that everyone processes information in a different way. What was right for me was not right for others. It made me understand that each of us is different, so each of our truths are different, and yes, that means each of our paths is different. This is why it is so important to understand your own Simple Truth and to know where your path leads. It makes staying on it so much easier.

The path to living your own Simple Truth is not dictated by the big decisions you have to make every once in a while, but by the little choices you make every day. Those are the things that will lead your life in the right direction. If you make good choices along the way, you will not be forced to make life-changing decisions. Your life will simply unfold as it should.

As its name implies, living your life by your own Simple Truth is predicated on two basic concepts:

> **Simplicity:** Strive to make your life as simple as possible, but no simpler. Reduce your needs, but not by so much that you no longer benefit from all the modern world has to offer.
>
> **Truth:** Be true to yourself and honest with others, no matter whom you find yourself to be.

These ideas are the essence behind the Simple Truth. If you learn to live simply and to be true to yourself, you will learn that you can override your old programming. You will gain the awareness you need to break through the self-doubt and clutter that derails your life. You will be empowered to make the right choices so that you can live your life the way YOU want to. It will enable you to slow down the world around you so that you can manage your life, YOUR way.

Understand Your Operating System

One hundred and forty thousand years ago our distant ancestors became, as best we can tell, human. At that time our operating systems were hard wired for survival. It took another 100,000 years before they started creating clothing, jewelry and art that we associate with modern humans. But even then, we were already hard wired for survival. Even though they had evolved to a point we refer to as modern humans, life for them was lived day by day based on their earlier programming.

Their actions were still a response to the world around them. Things happened, they responded, and they either lived or died based on that response. In a way life was relatively simple. They kept their eyes open and were constantly aware of their surroundings. They made choices quickly. If they made the right choice, they lived. If not, they died. It was drastic, but simple.

If something larger than them came out of the bushes they ran away to avoid being a meal. If they saw something smaller than them they ran toward it in the hopes of catching a meal. I can imagine one of our ancestors having a conversation that went something like this:

> "Oh, something is moving at the edge of this field. Perhaps it is a lion. I should run because it could be hungry and want to eat me. But wait, if it is a rabbit I could go to my village with dinner. Everybody would like me then. It does not look too big. My family is hungry. Should I wait and see if it is a lion? Think of what my tribe will think if I bring home a rabbit though. They will like me. I will wait and watch and perhaps bring dinner to my village. But I will also be ready to run..."

Their life was a constant state of fight or flight. In the 40,000 years since, the world has changed drastically. We now have homes with heating and glass windows. We have mugs with handles to keep our fingers from getting burned. We have hot water and markets. But the operating systems we rely on still work the same way they did 40,000 years ago. And therein lays the problem.

You no longer have hungry beasts lurking in the bushes. You no longer face life or death situations every day. The consequences of your actions are no longer instantaneous. Now they can take years and even decades to appear. Yet your brain and wiring don't work that way. Your brain and your wiring still look at the world around you and make split-second decisions as if your life depended on it. They don't allow you to take time to think about your actions. That means that the decisions you make are not always in your best interest, especially over the long-term.

How many times have you had a conversation in your own head that sounds something like this?

> "Oh look, a sign for a fifty percent sale. I should go in and buy something. I don't really need anything, but whatever they have is half off. It may make me late for my date, but if I show up with a new pair of shoes – now that would impress him. Besides he'll understand; and it is 50% off! Let me at least take a look. There's no harm in looking. Besides, I'll keep an eye on my watch..."

I think we can all agree that this is not a life or death situation. But our brains still treat it as if it was. We get caught up in the moment and focus on the issue in front of us. We put ourselves into a virtual tunnel where everything else fades away. Our focus narrows to the immediate issue, in this case, a 50% off sale. We then jump to a decision the same way that our ancestors did when they saw the leaves rustling at the far end of a field. We fail to think about the consequences of our actions.

Even though you say you will watch the time. Once you are in your bubble, hours can pass without notice. And that date you had? He may not understand why you showed up an hour late with shopping bags in hand. He may even be upset that he is so low on your list of priorities that you would make him wait without so much as a second thought. So not only are you buying things that you don't really need. You're making the rest of your evening and life worse because of a single bad choice. Once again, your short term response won out, to the detriment of the long-term.

It's not just women that do this. Men are just as guilty. Consider a conversation with yourself that sounded like this?

> "Oh look, a sign for a sale on big screen television sets. I don't really have the money, and I already have a smaller set, but man, wouldn't the guys be impressed. Besides, I can put it on credit. I'm not really sure how that all works, but if I don't have to pay for ninety days, then I don't have to worry for three months. I am sure I can figure out how to pay for it by then. My wife may shout about college and all, but she'll understand; and it is 50% off! Let me at least take a look. There's no harm in looking..."

Meanwhile your wife or girlfriend may be trying to figure out why she is waiting home alone on such a beautiful day when you made plans to go for a long hike together.

My point here is not to say "don't buy shoes on sale." It is not to say "don't buy a new television." It is to say your old programming puts you in a position to make flash decisions as if your lives depended on them, when it simply doesn't.

Your body and brain don't know you now live in a concrete jungle with a whole new set of concerns. They don't realize there are no wild animals lurking in the bush. They also don't know that just because you survive an encounter with an On Sale sign today, doesn't mean the consequences of your purchase will not have an impact on your credit for years to come.

If you can slow down your decision making process, if you can hit the pause button in your programming so that you can consider their long-term impact, then you can gain control of your life. This is exactly why you need to bring your programming up to date and evolve the way you think and make decisions.

What may seem like a simple choice now has ripples that will continue to affect your life for years to come. Learning how to be mindful of your actions is one part of achieving this. It does not mean you have to have a long, inner dialogue every time you want to do something or buy something. But it does require you to be aware, so that you can act in a way that is in your best interest, not in the interest of your old programming, or of the outside world.

> ***Simple Truth***
>
> *Don't blame your lack of progress on the distractions that fill your days. Rise from bed and take a chance at your life. This day is yours if you want it.*

Meet the YOU Inside of You

The first step in finding your own Simple Truth lies in recognizing that the "you" everyone sees and knows is not the real "YOU" that you were born to be.

Have you ever had a conversation that started inside your head while you were talking to someone? As if you were observing yourself from outside your body, even as you smiled and nodded at their banter? Perhaps it went something like this:

> Wow, this is a really dull conversation. I'm smiling, but I have no interest in this person in front of me. Just keep nodding and they will think I'm engaged. Hey, what about those people over there? It looks like they're having fun. Those are the kind of people I want to be a part of. Why can't I be over there instead of trapped with this person? Does this person really think I am fascinated with his office stories? Is this fake smile really working this well? I need to remember this for some dates in the future.

In that moment, you may not have consciously realized it, but you saw that there was someone else in your life. You became aware that the "you" everyone sees on the outside, is not necessarily the YOU who is the real force behind the person they know. The YOU who spoke to you is a part of your larger being, and someone you most definitely need to know.

Just realizing that YOU exist is an amazing step in your personal evolution. Once you question who you are on the outside, you cannot help but realize that deep down inside the real YOU, the consciousness that lives on the inside, is probably very different than the "you" most people see on the outside.

Recognizing the YOU on the inside is the key to finding your own Simple Truth. It is also the key to removing all of the distractions in your life that have prevented you from being who YOU really are.

So who is the YOU that I refer to? It is the same energy that every religion acknowledges. Some call it your soul, others your spirit, others your ki. Regardless of the name it is the reason that no matter where you go YOU will always be the same deep down inside. No matter what outfit you wear or what face you put on YOU will always be YOU.

This is important to understand, because evolving does not mean changing who YOU are at your core. Quite the opposite, it means tearing away all of the detritus that has been layered on top of the real YOU and has, somewhere along the way, created the person everyone knows you to be. Personal evolution means learning how to use your Simple Truth in order to be true to YOURSELF and to live your own dharma.

Now that you understand one of the most important concepts behind your personal evolution, you need to also understand that everything changes all the time. You change, your friends change, the world around you changes. You need to be comfortable with this idea, as it will free you from old attachments and enable you to constantly evolve. It will also reduce the stress you have from the changes that occur.

As the world changes around you, the opportunities that are presented to you will change with it. If you can calmly acknowledge those changes, accept them, and move forward, you can manage your life more easily and with less stress.

This is why it is so important to know who you are and to be true to YOURSELF. As long as you are true to the real YOU, the world can change around you, and YOU will still be fine.

Along your journey to living your own Simple Truth you will meet people who will help you. You will also meet people who will hinder you. Interacting with each honestly is essential to your growth and to maintaining your course in life. Only when you are not true, when you lie, when you cheat, when you steal, will you hurt yourself and hinder your own growth.

This leads me to the three basic concepts you need to know in order to live your life by your own Simple Truth. They will provide you with a jumping off point for the rest of your life.

Accept who YOU are, for better or worse. No matter how hard you try, YOU will always be there. So meet YOURSELF and learn who YOU are to live the life you love.

Be true to yourself, no matter where you go. Be ready to put your foot down. Be ready to walk away. But also be ready to embrace YOURSELF and your Simple Truth.

Recognize that the only constant in life is change, Learn to welcome change. It is a universal constant. Embrace it; evoke it, but only to follow your own Simple Truth.

Now that you understand the basics behind the Simple Truth, it is time to learn how you can bring this powerful idea into your life. If you are ready to start living YOUR life and creating a life you love, then you will need to start deleting some of the old programs and habits that are holding you back. You need to overcome the hurdles that are preventing you from getting to where you want to go. Only after you have torn down the barriers that are holding you back can you begin to build yourself up and enjoy the life that you were meant to live.

These are the four steps that will show you how you do it.

Four Steps to Your Personal Evolution

For most people the thought of change is scary. It should be. Change implies that you have done something wrong. It suggests that you need to get in line and start doing things the "right" way. Well, guess what, there is no "right" way to live your life. There is only YOUR way. After all, it is YOUR life and you need to start living it in a way that is in line with who YOU are. If you don't, you may just find yourself waking up on a hospital bed one day wondering why you spent all that time living your life the way someone else wanted you to live it, chasing after someone else's dreams, only to find out that in the end they were not really all that important to you in the first place.

My guess is that you have probably tried living your life their way, the "right" way. I am also guessing that their way still hasn't given you the life you want. Don't worry you're not the first one to be where you are. Just look at Wall Street, or Hollywood, or Madison Avenue. Look at the moguls in Detroit or the oilmen in Houston. Everywhere around you people have run after an image of the life they thought they should be living.

They have sacrificed their lives to fit someone else's dreams, and very few of them are even close to being happy. Don't get me wrong. There is nothing wrong with wealth. But wealth is not happiness. Nor should it be the sole motivator in your life.

> ***Simple Truth***
>
> *The only constant in this world is change. If you want to be happy learn to welcome it, embrace it, and to love it. For change is inevitable.*

If you have tried to live your life by someone else's rules, then you know what it's like. You can do it for a while. But sooner or later, you will realize it is not YOUR life. Now is the time to try something different. Now is the time to start living the life you want to live. Forget about changing who you are to fit someone else's expectations. Forget about molding yourself to someone else's idea of who you should be. Instead, think about growing and evolving on a personal level so that you can live the life you want to live; one that is in YOUR best interest.

There is nothing wrong with looking out for your own best interest. There is nothing wrong with putting yourself first. After all, this is your life. Just don't sacrifice someone else's well being for your own. Keep in mind that everyone else has their own lives too. So when you act, keep words like compassion, karma, and respect in mind. Those concepts will never prevent you from being YOU. In fact, they will more than likely help you do so. As you will see, if you live in a way that is true to YOURSELF you will find that YOUR best interests really are in accord with everyone else's interests. You will see that living in a compassionate and respectful way is actually in line with everyone's Simple Truth.

So let's talk about YOU. At your core is the essence of the person you were born to be. This is your original self, with all of your faults and advantages. This is the person you need to get back to being if you truly want to live the life you love. This is the real YOU.

Don't be afraid of that person. It is already a part of who you are. You are not changing. You are just reuniting with your original self. You will still laugh at all the jokes you love to laugh at and cry at all the movies you love to cry at. The difference is that you will do them without feeling guilt or remorse about your emotions.

When you evolve, you simply learn to embrace all the different parts of yourself. You gain the ability to filter through the influences and the noise of the outside world so that you can manage your relationship with the people and the world around you, so that you can shape your life into the one you love.

The best part of evolving on a personal level is that you do not have to have brain surgery to do it. You do not need to hook up any wires or take a red pill to get it started. You do not need to live in a monastery or give up your worldly possessions. You do not need to renounce your beliefs or drink strange teas. All you need to do is to learn how to use the tools you already have inside of you. You just need to learn how to stay true to your own Simple Truth.

When you start living by your own Simple Truth you will learn how much you are influenced by the outside world. As you continue down your path you will learn more about yourself and how you interact with the world around you. You will also learn how to use a simple process called CaRE to help you move your life into a direction you want it to go.

As you evolve those around you will notice the changes. You will begin to see that many of your old patterns just aren't there anymore. Others may find they can't antagonize you like they used to while you start to recognize their efforts to push your buttons for what they are:

> **First:** You will find greater comfort as you silence your inner voice and remove the influences of the outside world so that you can find your own Simple Truth. Not the truth someone else has impressed upon you.
>
> **Second:** You will learn to use mindfulness and meditation in order to find your Simple Truth and live the life you want to live.
>
> **Third:** You will gain greater control over the choices you make every day with a program called CaRE so that you can create the life you want and reach the destiny inside of you.
>
> **Fourth:** You will learn to live mindfully to maintain your focus in your life in order to realize your dreams.

Each of these stages is a step forward in your own journey of self realization and actualization. Each will transform your life. They will also help you renew your relationship with the people and the world around you. They will help you peel away all of the distractions that do not support your own Simple Truth so that you spend less time worrying and more time doing; less time paralyzed and more time taking your life back.

The Simple Truth is not a once a week exercise or a sometime escape. It is the start of an ongoing transformation based on your own personal needs. It will help you to wake up excited by the opportunities of every day. It will guide you as the path unfolds before you. It is not always an easy journey, but it will bring you fulfillment, not

---

Simple Truth

Do not worry about what could be in the future or what was in the past. Just concern yourself with the present. The rest will figure itself out.

---

just when you arrive to where you are going, but throughout your entire adventure.

The one thing I can promise you is that at some point you will look back and think to yourself "How did I ever think that old life was a good one? It wasn't even me." You will also look ahead and realize that you now have a life that is worth living every second to the fullest of your ability. Living the Simple Truth reminds me of that old saying – "the worst day fishing is better than the best at the office." That has never been truer than with the Simple Truth.

Step 1:

Remove Your Outside Influences

Every time some outside stimulus affects you, your natural reaction is to jump to a decision quickly. You respond before you really have the chance to think through your actions. You react as if your very survival is on the line, when it is simply not. This is your old programming at work. It is trying to save your life, even when your life is not in danger.

With the conveniences of the modern world, you should be living a very relaxed life at this point, able to enjoy the fruits of more than 140,000 years of progress. But you aren't. You cannot relax for one simple reason. Your programming is still responding to the outside world just like it did when modern man appeared 40,000 years ago; in fight or flight mode.

Look around. You have food, wrapped and ready to go. You have glass in your windows to keep the temperature just right while letting light in. You have a universe of information available at the touch of your fingertips. You also have a level of stress and distraction that your ancestors never experienced, let alone your grandparents. The killers of today, stress, cancer, diabetes, were not even known when you were hard wired for a completely different type of survival. Much of this comes from your response to the outside world. Imagine how enjoyable your life could be if you could just reduce the noise by a small percentage.

It is estimated that you see more than three thousand advertising and marketing messages every day. Nobody has even tried to calculate how many more distractions come through your mobile phone or via email; and that doesn't even start to consider the speed of oncoming cars, people walking down the street, clients that want 24/7 attention, or an up-to-the minute news cycle that is brought to you by hundreds of television stations, newspapers and internet websites. It is no wonder that you live in a constant state of stress. Your body is trying to keep up with modern survival using an outdated operating system; and it simply can't.

On the one hand your ancestors created the world you live in. On the other hand it is a world that your body and brain were just not built for. You are not wired for a wired world; and that has created the constant anxiety, the feeling of inadequacy, the need to strive for more, and the constant feeling of failure you experience every day. It is not because you are doing the wrong things. It is because no matter how much you do or how fast you work, you are still wired with a 140,000 year old operating system.

Like any computer, before you can upload a new program you have to delete the old one that is causing the problems. The same is true of the programs that are now directing your life. You know these as the old patterns and habits that have been running your life and holding you back. They are your need to jump to a response, your need for acceptance as well as the old prejudices, fears and desires that have kept you from being true to YOURSELF. Once these are gone you will be free to access your own Simple Truth and upload a new way to live.

In order to free yourself from the outside influences that have controlled much of your life you need to start by overriding six old programs. As you will see, without them, you will be better able to simplify your life, reduce your stress and identify your own Simple Truth. All of which is essential to creating the life you love.

This chapter, what I call Step 1, walks you through each of these programs. Approach them one at a time and you will see some remarkable breakthroughs. Just think of these as deeply embedded and outdated programs that simply need to go. Yes, eliminating them requires persistence, but once you do, you will be amazed at how great it feels to be able to truly live your life based on what YOU want.

> ***Simple Truth***
>
> *You don't have to be ashamed of your impulses. Nor do you have to act on them.*

They are far less mysterious than you may think. In fact you will find life is instantly more manageable without them. As you start to clean out your old software and begin to reprogram the way you manage your life, you will find a greater awareness of who YOU are. You may also find that the person you thought you wanted to be will change, sometimes drastically. It is because as your awareness of the world around increases, the noise in your life will start to fade away leaving you to choose who you want to be.

They are:

Silence your negative inner voice

Increase your self-awareness

Overcome the expectations of others

Embrace your faults

Ignore the call of advertising & consumerism

Focus your unfocused mind

For some of you, overcoming these obstacles may be the first time you will open your eyes and truly see yourself and the world as it is. This is not always easy, but it is part of growing, of maturing, and of evolving. By acknowledging the realities of the real world around you, you will learn how to refocus your attention on those things that truly matter to you. It is a part of your evolution to the person YOU were meant to be.

Silence Your Negative Inner Voice

How many times do you wake up to your inner voice? How many times are you kept awake by it? You know the one. That nagging, questioning, berating voice that comes up without regard to where you are or what you are doing. For most of you, it is the first thing you hear in the morning and the last thing you hear before drifting off to sleep.

Do you remember the last time you heard your inner voice? I'm guessing that it was not positive. It was most likely negative, pointing out a fault or issue that had been nagging at your subconscious. If you were having a good day, it may have come as a barrage of concerns that didn't let up. If you were having a bad day, it may have sounded like a deafening roar of failure.

Rarely is your inner voice optimistic. It does not care what you are thinking about, nor is it interested in starting a conversation. There is no back and forth with your inner voice. Let's face it your inner voice wants to talk and keep to its own agenda rather than engage in a real conversation. It simply wants to be heard.

As soon as you take the bait and respond to whatever it is saying, your inner voice will most likely change its position or jump to a new topic altogether. You're left dazzled by the speed at which it eludes a dialogue. It is as if at some point you adopted a nagging, snoopy neighbor that pops their head into your home whenever they feel like it. More often than not when you are alone, but even if you're in the middle of a conversation with someone else it can be there – ready to point out if you're slouching or have a hair out of place. If you get tongue tied, that will only make it worse.

Forty thousand years ago, that voice of worry helped our ancestors survive. It pointed out things that were not right. Today it still does that. Only without the dangers of the outside world, it quickly turns its attention inward, to you.

The next time you are walking down the street or along a path, listen to how quickly your inner voice starts to narrate your walk. It may start out by pointing to everything that you see around you. It might sound something like this:

> "Wow, what a beautiful day this has turned out to be. Look at the blue sky, and look at that rooftop. It has a cornice that I'm sure most people never look up to see. Everybody is out today. Look, that person is walking a dog. Is it a terrier? A boxer? Oh, I don't know what it is, but Steve has a dog like it. I should call Steve. I wonder what he's doing now. Oh, what is that smell? Pizza? I should stop and get some. I wonder if it's as good as the kind I used to get as a kid. It's probably not as good. Besides the carbs are just something I don't need right now. But I am walking, which is good for me. I wonder if the people in LA walk as much as a New Yorker walks? There's no way they're in as a good shape as New Yorkers. They drive, we walk, every day."

On it goes, in an endless narration of your life. Not that your life needs a narration today, but that is what it does. That is how it was programmed. It is almost as if your brain is trying to comfort itself. It is as if your brain is acknowledging everything around you to reassure itself that nothing is out of place and that you're free from danger. It categorizes everything you see, hear, smell and taste. Then it starts to associate everything in your present environment to your memory to make sure your world is okay.

It doesn't know that you no longer live in the primordial forests of your ancestors. Without the dangers your ancestors faced, your survival instincts are left looking for things to do. So your instincts turn themselves to the next best thing. Instead of looking around you for anything that might be out of place, your mind turns its attention inward, to you. The end result is that your old programming, once focused on your survival, starts to act like some kind of self-induced analysis that never stops. Even when you're safely at home and in bed your brain continues to work as it always has. Only now it is analyzing you rather than the world around you. As we all know, the only thing worse than having your life narrated while you live it, is to have your life analyzed when you are trying to take a break from it.

To break this cycle, you need to become aware of your inner voice and learn to recognize it when it speaks up. You don't need to argue with it or engage with it. You just have to recognize it. You need to learn what it sounds like and remember the tone it takes. You also need to remember how you are feeling when it rises up.

It usually happens when you have let your guard down or are feeling vulnerable. For some it may amplify during a stressful situation, like just before a presentation. For others it may amplify just when you want to relax or drift off in a peaceful sleep. Sometimes it happens in the middle of a meeting when you are overwhelmed, or when you are feeling nervous about a date you've found yourself on. Regardless of where you are, it sticks to the same tactics. It may start with a narrative of where you are, only to turn into a review of your life. Or it may point out a fault you noticed before you left home and drill down into it, making it seem larger and larger than it really is.

Have you ever had a conversation like this going on in your head?

> "Was it just me, or did Brad act oddly in the hall today? He wasn't as friendly as he's been in the past. When was the last time I saw him? I don't think I did anything. I should call him and see. But if I do and nothing's wrong he will think something's going on with me. And that will make him think I'm interested. That could be wonderful. But there's no way he's interested. Besides we work together. I've also got to lose a few before I approach him. I really do. I just need to pull back on the snacks. Oh, and get back to yoga again. It's great when I do it, but I'm just not a morning person. I'm such a loser; I can't even get to yoga in the morning. He's not going to go out with a loser..."

On it goes well into the morning or into your meeting. It is an inner dialogue over events and issues that you have no control over. Usually in such an open ended way that there is no easy way to resolve it, or to think through all of the ways in which the future could play out. But there you are, rolling around in bed, or staring mindlessly as your meeting goes on around you, unable to focus or sleep as your mind rambles on about anything and everything it wants to.

The next time you hear it, ask yourself, if your inner voice was an actual person would they be your friend? Would you ever hang out with him or her? The answer is most likely no. You would not call your inner voice to get together on the weekend. You would not ruin a beautiful day with their ceaseless narration. You would not listen to them pointing out all of your faults or changing the subject every time you tried to have a dialogue.

Your inner voice is really like a bad officemate from the next cubicle or a nosy neighbor. It is someone you are forced to live with but not someone you would take a call from. So if your inner voice is not someone you would want as a friend, why do you keep giving it a voice in your life? More important, how can you get it to leave you alone?

The answer is simple. If your inner voice were a person, you would politely ignore them until they left; which is exactly what you should do with your inner voice. If you learn to ignore your inner voice it will eventually tone itself down until it eventually fades away. And yes, this is easier than you may think. It just takes focus and breathing.

So start by becoming aware of your own inner voice. Don't engage it; just listen to it in an unattached way. Once you have trained yourself to be aware of it, then you can start to use a simple mindfulness technique to override its banter which will give you the power to turn it down.

The next time you hear your inner voice comment on something you have done, stop for a moment. Listen to it. Don't interrupt it; just be aware that it is there. Listen to it without engaging it. You will want to. But stop yourself. Simply say to yourself, "stop" every time you do.

Notice several things about its monologue. First, it never stops talking <u>at</u> you. Second, it does not want a dialogue, it simply wants to talk. Know that it was initially programmed to be the point-person in your life, to watch out for you. So that is what it does.

It may start out with a commentary on the world around you. It may take the lead from something that is on your mind. Either way, from there your inner voice is off and running. If you do not respond it may start a running dialogue of the most mundane things going on around you until finally you give in. Yet once you acknowledge it, it quickly changes the subject to a critical monologue on what you are more often than not, doing wrong. It may start its conversation in the present, but quickly changes subjects about hypothetical events that may, or may not happen. It loves to point out how you could have handled something better in the past, or how you could handle it better in the future. All of which comes from a much skewed perspective. If you do prove it wrong, it changes the subject so that it is once again on top; because that is where it is programmed to be.

As it tries to do what it is programmed to do, it will prevent you from reflecting on the positive aspects of your life and on the things you are doing right. It will keep you from achieving the things that you want to achieve. It is not inherently evil. It is simply an old program that has lasted far beyond its usefulness.

Now that you have listened to it and learned how it works, the next time you hear it, do exactly what it is preventing you from doing – living in the here and now. Instead of taking the bait and responding, treat it like an annoying roommate. Simply smile. Physically smile, and say hello to it inside your own head.

Really, say "hello. I missed you." It may sound silly, but it will make your inner voice pause. It will also allow you to treat it like a person – albeit a very annoying person.

Next, take a deep cleansing breath[2], and as you exhale say the word you want to think about. If you are in bed and want to go to sleep, repeat the word "sleep" with every breath and focus on it. Even spell the word, one letter at a time, with every slow inhale and every slow exhale. If you are out for a walk, say the word "walk" and acknowledge the world around you. Spell it with every breath. If it is daytime, take some time to acknowledge the sun, the clouds, the trees or the sidewalk. If it is night, take the time to look at the moon, the stars, or the dark sky. Just be sure to live in the here and now.

Your inner voice will try to start again. It will try to distract you. That's okay. Acknowledge the fact that you just got distracted and then go back breathing and repeating your word. By focusing on your word or the physical world around you, your inner voice will eventually fade into the background. You will find your own thoughts will shift and focus on the here and now – the present. Not the world your inner voice wants you to live in.

This simple exercise of breathing and being mindful of yourself and the world around you will help you control your inner voice. It will help you change your relationship to it. It is the first step in directing your life and doing what you want to do. This may seem like such a simple exercise[3], but it has far reaching effects. Once you become comfortable with it, it can

---

2 See chapter two to learn how to breathe properly and how to take a cleansing breath.

3 Mindfulness techniques are detailed later in the book. For now use this technique to reduce the influences in your life and free you of clutter so that you can grow.

help you to stop worrying about events and issues that are outside of your control so that you can focus your energy on the things that you can actually impact.

This combination of breathing and more focused awareness is the key to freeing yourself from your incessant inner voice. It is also the key to freeing yourself from the traps that your old programming has created for you. By stepping back from the dialogue of your inner voice, by acknowledging where it comes from, and by not empowering it with the control it wants, you will set yourself free. You will be amazed how quickly your inner voice will quiet down and eventually leave you alone altogether. You will also be amazed at how you can apply this same technique to other parts of your life – even to people.

So, the next time you hear your inner voice rise up inside of you. Stop and acknowledge it. Do not respond to it. Just listen to what it is saying. Be aware that you are listening to it as if it were another person at your place of work. Smile and breathe. If it is talking about future events, be aware that you have no control over them, and tell it so. Tell it "I can only influence those events I know to be true. Not those I am guessing at." If it is telling you about the world around you, stop, smile, breathe slowly and deeply, and see the world that is around you without the narration of your inner voice.

Understand that:

Your inner voice is an old program – it was a way for your old operating system to make sense of the world your ancestors lived in. But today it is a program that you need to manage rather than allow it to manage you, if you are to grow and evolve past it.

Your inner voice is not you – It is a dialogue that is based on everything that you see, that you hear, and that you feel. It is a response that your old operating system is having while it tries to make sense of the modern world. It is not useless, but it should no longer be in control of your life. Most important, it is not YOU, nor is it YOUR dialogue.

Silence your inner voice – This is the first step to living YOUR life. Silencing your inner voice will help you train your mind in a way that will empower you throughout your journey.

Increase Your Self-Awareness

Have you ever asked yourself "Who am I?" It sounds like a simple question. But for most of us it is anything but simple. Most of you may ask the question, but then allow yourself to get distracted before you ever find the answer. Others may quit the inevitable line of questioning that follows because it becomes a longer process than you had imagined.

The reason this is a larger question than it appears is because your life is constantly changing. You are constantly being influenced by the world and the people around you. So you change with it. It is not necessarily a bad thing it is simply a part of living in today's world.

The people around you want you to act in a certain way. Even with the best of intentions they look at your life through their own expectations. They push you to reach for the same goals they are after. They have their own dreams and expectations, but unfortunately, most of what they want is not what you want. The result is good advice for them, but bad advice for you.

To complicate things even further, once said their advice doesn't just go away. It stays with you. It causes you to doubt and judge yourself well into the future. It is one reason why as you mature you change. Not into the person you were born to be, but into the person society and the people around you want you to be. This is why when you ask yourself "who am I," you don't see the real YOU at first, but the "you" that "YOU" have come to be. There is nobody to blame for this. It is not anyone's fault. But it is something to be aware of, so that you can stop living everyone else's life and start living your own.

Simple Truth

Don't change who you are. Evolve into the person YOU were meant to be.

When I talk about finding your own Simple Truth, I am talking about finding the essence of who you were when you first entered the world, and before all of the outside influences became layered on top of you. Deep down inside, you still are that person. But if you are to be truly happy you need to return to your natural self, your own Simple Truth.

Becoming self aware is the first step to finding the real YOU beneath all of those layers. Once you do, you will still need to work to make a living. You will still need to take care of life's responsibilities. But instead of taking a job you don't want, you can start focusing on a job, on friends, and on a lifestyle that will feed your own Simple Truth and truly make you happy. You can, in effect, return to the path you were originally put on when you came into this world, and start learning the lessons you were put here to learn.

For most of you your unhappiness is not due to the generalities of your life, but to the details of your life. Perhaps your relationship no longer feeds you, perhaps your job has added the wrong kind of stress to your days, perhaps your friends are not supporting the real YOU. More than likely it is a combination of all of these things. The good news is at some point you gained enough experience in life to want to refine the details of your life in order to create a life you not just enjoy, but love.

To start, let's not focus on changing who you are, but instead focus on refining the details of your life. If you can refine the details of your life, you don't' have to change who you are. Instead, you can advance specific parts of your life so that they support the person you were meant to be; and in doing so, create a life that makes you happy. So ask yourself that simple question, "Who am I?"

Take a moment to look in the mirror. Are you the person staring back at you? I doubt it. The face looking back at you is not really you. It is a reflection of you at this moment in time. When I am well rested and feeling great about myself, the face I see in the mirror glows with confidence. When I am exhausted and worn out, the face in the mirror is tired and insecure. The face I see in the mirror changes depending on my mood and my perception of the world around me. It does for all of us. So the person you see in the mirror is not who you really are. It is an image, a reflection of the person you are at the moment you stare at it.

In the same way if someone were to look at my driver's license or my Facebook profile they are really seeing a snapshot of me at a point in my life. If someone saw my information, they might say "Oh, you're Jeff Cannon. You live at such and such an address and you are so many years old." But is that really me? Does any of that reflect my views, my beliefs, or my character? The answer is no. All of those bits of data are just labels. They are a way to identify me from the masses of people out there.

If you were to Google "Jeff Cannon" you would find hundreds of people with the same name, but each of us with a very different and unique makeup. Believe me, I've looked. So you see you are more than your name or your image. You are a very unique collection of ideas and attitudes, of experiences and dreams, of hopes and aspirations. You are different from anyone else because you have made choices in your life that nobody else has made. Some have been right, many have been wrong, but each one has helped to create the person everyone has come to know.

Simple Truth

Happiness is not a goal. It is the result of living your life the right way.

Just as important as your past choices, are your dreams for the future. Your hopes and dreams cause you to make choices that nobody else will make. All of those will continue to change you as time marches on. Tomorrow you will be slightly different than you are today. Just as you are now different than the person you were ten years ago. That is the beauty of life. It always changes.

It is also why it is important to recognize that the real YOU is not defined by the clothes you wear or the things you own. YOU are defined by the attitudes you have toward yourself and toward others. The real YOU is defined by how you interact with the world, and the people, around you. Are you kind? Are you compassionate? Are you driven? Are you spiritual? Are you fair? These are the questions to ask yourself, because they define who YOU are. Those are the idiosyncrasies that truly characterize you. And if you know who YOU are, then no matter where you go, you will always have a rock that you can return to. You will have your own Simple Truth to come back to.

This is why it is so important to become aware of who YOU are, of what is important to YOU. Call it a point of reference for yourself so that you can put a stake in the ground at any point in time and say, "This is who I am." Once you know yourself, you can start to shape a life that is in line with the person you really are instead of the person others want you to be.

Being YOU is what will make you happy. It will help you attain the things that really matter to you and will help you create a life you love. With your own Simple Truth as a guideline, you can start making the right choices that will keep you on your right path no matter where you end up wanting to go.[4]

Once you have your stake in the ground you can easily set a direction for your life so that every step you take from there on will get closer to your own Simple Truth. Every choice you make will become an opportunity to nudge your life back in the right direction and guide you to the person you want to be. But before you do any of this, you need to become aware of yourself, because only then can you set the direction for your personal evolution.

In life, most of you go through your daily routine on auto-pilot. I know I did. You wake up, you make coffee, you go to work and you come home. Few of you actually think about what you are doing on a day-to-day basis let alone how those actions fit into your larger mission in life. In a way living like this is like living in a dream. Only instead of it being YOUR dream, it is someone else's. A dream based on the wishes of other people as well as your desire to fit into the world we all live in.

Don't worry, we are about to transform that. You will notice I say transform and evolve instead of change. There is a reason for this. Change implies it will happen quickly. Evolution and

---

4 Later on we will actually do an exercise of discovery, but for now, just understand the principle behind the process.

transformation imply a shift that happens over time. A sharp change can do more harm than good. A gradual shift can be finessed and adjusted along the way. It can be integrated slowly into your life, so that you can still enjoy your life as you move it in the direction you want to go.

Have you ever had inner conversations like these?

> Wow, I'd love to go vegan. But it's a little crunchy for my friends. What if Janice found out? She would never let up. She'd tease me for days. I could just not tell them. But what happens when we all go out for dinner? No, I'll just do the vegan thing when I'm at home. That way it will just keep it easy.

Or:

> If I had the chance to do it all over, I would have become a graphic designer. I'm pretty good at design and I love helping people turn their ideas into something tangible. But if I did, what would I do with my college degree? It would mean I wasted four years of my life studying law.

Or:

> Wow, Uncle Stephens is a self-made man. Everyone in the family looks up to him. He's the guy to beat. That was a nice job offer I got. But forget about working with a large company. I've got to strike out on my own if I want to be somebody I can be proud of.

Each of these decisions has one thing in common. They are all influenced by the wants, needs, and dreams of others. It doesn't matter if you are the one ultimately putting pressure on yourself. The pressure stems from the same place – the people and the world around you. No matter how well meaning those people are, when you make a decision based on their needs, you are not making the right decisions for YOU.

In order to move beyond the outside influences of your life, your own Simple Truth needs to be the "why" behind the "what" that you are doing. Only then can you put your automatic programming on pause and make the kind of decisions that will keep your life on the path YOU want to go.

Being “aware” or being “mindful” of yourself and the world around you is the best way to do this. It simply means that you are living in the present moment with an understanding of your decisions. That you are not living your life based on the fears and influences of your past or in anticipation of the future. It means recognizing the "why" behind the "what" that you are doing. So that you can start to live in the modern world you now find yourself in, instead of the prehistoric world you were programmed for.

Having a heightened awareness gives you the ability to pause your decision making process[5] so that you can make good life choices based on longer term thinking rather than immediate gratification. It enables you to make the kind of choices that will help you achieve what YOU want out of life, not what your family or your friends want for you.

There is a wonderful moment in the film, the Matrix, when the lead character is physically unplugged from the computer that was his life. He becomes truly aware of the world around him for the first time in his existence. When he opens his eyes and sees the real world around him it is a traumatic experience. But for the first time he is able to make decisions based on the reality of his present moment, rather than on the impressions he has lived by.

---

[5] I will introduce you to a process called Living with CaRE later in this book that will give you the pause button to your life.

It will be no less dramatic for you. When you become aware of how your actions have been influenced by old habits, by the media, or by someone you know and even respect, you will start to see how greatly your decisions have been, and are, influenced by the world around you.

Don't panic. Just take a deep breath. At this point, being aware does not mean taking action. The time will come for that. For now, simply learn to be aware when your inner voice acts up. Be aware when your emotions start to rise and influence your decisions. Be aware when an outside event triggers a response within you. Most important, look back at the decisions you have made to see when your actions were driven by habit, rather than a conscious thought.

When a driver cuts you off and your instinct throws you into a rage, you need to be aware how you responded without thinking. When a political candidate makes you angry, you need to be aware that they are manipulating you with a well planned and tested agenda, the specific intent of which is to make you angry and boost their poll results. When you see a sale sign or an advertisement, be aware of your reaction to their message and of your desire to buy.

Being aware of how you respond to the world around you will enable you to separate yourself from an event so that you can actively decide whether to engage in it or to move past it. Being aware enables you to make your own decisions based on what is best for YOU rather than on what your old habits or programming are telling you to do.

As an exercise, start with something simple like just being aware of the world around you when you take a walk. Set some time aside to go for a slow, unhurried walk and simply name the things that you see. Narrate your walk for yourself and be aware of the world with every step you take.

You may feel self conscious or even foolish at first. That's okay. Simply breathe slowly and deeply and acknowledge that you feel that way. Just say to yourself, "I feel really stupid doing this." But then also acknowledge what you are doing by saying, "I am being aware of the world around me." Then go back to naming the world that you are walking through.

When you order lunch, take a moment to think about what you want before you order. Make sure you are not just ordering the same thing you had yesterday and the day before, but really consider what you <u>want</u>. Slow down your world if you have to; let the person behind you go ahead so that you can actually think through your order. In each of these exercises you are increasing your awareness of yourself and the world around you. This simple step may actually be a shock when you realize how little you actually think, rather than do. It will help you to start evolving the way you view the world and yourself.

Do this for a week. Just observe the world. As you do, try to also become aware of your own emotions. The next time you feel yourself getting angry, pause and take three deep breaths. Acknowledge that your emotions are changing and that you are changing because of it. Don't comment on them. Simply take another breath and understand what is going on in your own mind and body.

When something happens that affects you ask yourself, "Am I getting angry?" "Am I feeling nervous?" "Am I getting aroused?" "Do I want to strike out at someone?" "Do I want to hug someone?" Do not worry about what to do next. Just be aware that you are having a new emotion and acknowledge how that makes you feel. We will deal with next steps later in this book. For now, just start to take notice of yourself and the world around you.

Once you begin this process you will be amazed at how much you have lived your life in a robotic fog. You will also begin to see how large an impact a small change in your awareness of the world around you can have on your life.

Overcome the Expectations of Others

As you increase your awareness of the world around you and of yourself, you will become increasingly aware of the actions of others. You will start to realize how others influence your own actions. Most of these interactions do not end in the screaming matches and fights that today's media loves to show. More often they come in the form of subtle comments, asides and put-downs. They are hidden in casual conversation and behind polite smiles. They come in the downward looks of a disapproving family member or the blank stare of a boss or co-worker. They are insults veiled by little statements like "...oh, I'm just kidding" or "...the poor dear."

You have been taught to overlook these small comments and asides. You have been told to "turn the other cheek." So you tell yourself that you are above it all or are too polite to acknowledge it. You smile and laugh along with whatever is being said. You pretend to ignore it, but those small asides don't go away. They stay with you and build up. They layer on top of you like a gummy mess, and they never leave. If you don't take the time to remove them, they weigh you down and direct the choices you make and the life that you thought was your own.

Ever since you were a child, if someone was teasing you your teachers told you to go play in another part of the playground. That certainly made their job easier. It stopped the teasing at that moment, but rarely did that ever stop the problem. Instead, it just made you feel bad about yourself while someone else felt better about themselves – at least in the short term. This is not just a random coincidence. It is the effect of our programming.

This programming started early in our development as a species, based on our desire to just get along and our ability to overlook personal transgressions for the public good. It was a crucial part in our survival. It separated us from other primates and enabled our ancestors to hunt as a group so that we could down buffalo and wildebeests. It helped us create tribes and build societies.

Some scientists refer to this evolutionary process as self-breeding. In much the same way that we domesticated dogs and cats to be more lovable and docile, we self-bred ourselves to be able to work together and live alongside each other. Those able to live in the community were welcomed and shared in the advantages that brought. Those that were not, were ostracized and banished to live on their own. We still do this today. We send people to prisons. We have fraternities and sororities, clubs with velvet ropes and secret initiations. We isolate those that don't fit into our social structure. Want to get into a political party? Remember "it's not what you know, it's who you know."

It starts at an early age. You can see this programming at work in almost every school yard around the country. One child learns that if they push in the right way, politely and not violently, others will generally back down, wanting to avoid conflict. As they grow older, and as long as they don't go overboard with their manipulations, they learn how to use this mechanism to elevate their status and give them more control. In time, they learn how a little comment can keep others in their places. They learn how to bend the rules for their own gain. Of course the tradeoff is that someone else gets manipulated or hurt by their comments and asides.

If you were the one getting hurt, you probably started to think that for some reason you were simply "not in their league," or perhaps that you "just didn't measure up." The reality is, the people that learn to use control mechanisms like this are just as fragile and unsure of themselves as anyone else. They simply learned how to leverage a loophole in the programming to their advantage.

Simple Truth

Today will happen whether you rise or not. Greet it as loudly as you can and embrace whatever happens. After all, this day is there for you.

The Ten Commandments were introduced as laws for a peaceful society. They remain the basis for our laws today and still provide a wonderful baseline for how we should all act. As societies grew, manners were introduced as more refined guidelines for how people should behave. They continue to help us avoid confrontation and make the world a kinder, gentler place to live.

The key word here is guidelines, because they are not hard and fast rules to live by. If misused, they can prevent you from living your life as you were meant to live it. Once again, this is why you need to be aware when someone uses the concept of manners to belittle you as rude or uncouth, to undermine your self esteem. You need to identify which manners make sense to you and which ones you should think twice about. Holding the door open for someone, man or woman is simply a nice thing to do and shows that you care. Using the wrong fork at dinner shouldn't ruin your meal, even if the woman to your left is giving you a sidelong glance. Don't let her insecurities ruin the meal you are enjoying.

Those little comments over the years have added layers of fear, anger and resentment that now cover the real YOU. They prevent you from making decisions for fear of more reprisals in the future. They don't eat away at your core so much as they plaster it with self doubt. They are what create the person who now is living your life, the person most people know you to be.

Short circuiting the influence of others means doing more than stomping your foot and saying no. It means understanding who YOU are, what is important to YOU, and what YOU want to make of your life. It means recognizing that you do not need outside approval to be happy. It means re-training yourself so that you don't fall into that habit of responding instinctively. But that you take the time to respond properly – both on the outside, and on the inside.

At times we all need to do things we may not enjoy. It is the give and take of living in a larger society. The difference is less about how you respond to a given situation and more about how you feel when you respond. You can acquiesce to someone else's ideas without giving in. You can work together with someone without selling out. Being polite and complimenting someone to make them feel good is not selling out, unless you lose a part of yourself when you do so.

For you to find happiness and live the life you were born to live, you have to stop listening to the expectations of others. You have to set your own standards to live by based on what is important to you in life. Just be careful that you don't throw out the advice and counsel of others. You can learn a lot from those around you without feeling pressured to follow it. Learn as much as you can, but make sure the final decision is yours and yours alone.

This is the reason it is so important to be aware of who you really are, of what you really want, and to know when to pay attention to, and when to disregard the voices of those around you. How you listen to the voices of those around you is as important as what the voices say. The greater importance you place on them, the deeper they can go.

So be aware. Truly listen to what people are saying. Do not be afraid to smile, to take a deep breath, and to feel your own two feet on the ground before you say "Thank you for your input, but I prefer my way."

The power of knowing who you are, and of being aware of what your own life is meant to be is the power of being able to walk away smiling, knowing that you are living YOUR own life. After all, this is what life is all about. This is why you were put here – to live, to explore, to learn, and ultimately to grow.

Be Comfortable With Your Faults

In today's society, misrepresentations start at a very early age. Our television shows depict teenagers who have the insights of adults. Our magazines depict models air-brushed to unattainable perfection. Our movies depict stars who always say just the right lines in just the right tone. They are never fazed by anything around them.

The reality is that every line in a movie has been planned out, rehearsed, and then re-recorded in post-production to make sure it is perfect. And while you may understand that on paper, you still feel envious when you watch someone on the screen in front of you. They make you feel inadequate inside because even though you know it is fake your internal programming doesn't. It tells you that you can never live up to the unrealistic standards our society has created for everyone.

We all know life simply does not work the way it does on film. But your programming was created 40,000 before movies even existed. So deep down inside, your operating system doesn't know the difference. It looks at those people on screen as competition. It raises your bar so high that you feel you have to meet their level of perfection.

Your innate desire to find your place is the reason so many people are addicted to gossip columns – we all want to keep up with the competition. This is the reason we love to root for the underdog and cannot wait to rip into the celebrity who has stumbled. We want to fit into society, but we also don't want to lose our spot in the tribe."

In the celebrity driven world we live in, if anyone steps out of the "perfect box" there is a gossip magazine, blog or website just waiting to point out how imperfect someone is. Today you don't even need to be a star to be outted by a jealous interloper. In fact, you don't even need to be a celebrity for it to happen. It happens every day on Facebook, Twitter and any number of social networks. It is also why it is important that you learn to be aware of who you are and of the world around you.

You have to understand that you are not perfect. You never were. You never will be. Nobody is. The world is not perfect. There are cracks in the earth's surface, the continents are in a constant state of upheaval, and our cities are one step away from complete disrepair. Yet we keep working with what we have and we keep fixing them as best we can.

Understand that having faults is not the same as being a failure. It is simply being human.

You may be sick of hearing it, but each of you is great at something. It may not be math or English. It may not be computer programming or public speaking. It may not even be the job that you are currently paid to do. But there is something you are good at, you just need to find it and then know that the only standards you have to live up to are your own.

Einstein was a failure in school. He was also a pretty lousy mailman from all accounts. Picasso probably would never have been very good as an accountant. At the same time, some of the world's best financial minds could never paint like Rembrandt or Pollock no matter how hard they tried.

The people around you will always try to fit you into a convenient box. They want to be able to label you, no matter how wrong that label is. It simply makes them comfortable. But it can also destroy your life if you let it.

Schools start classifying students at an early age through testing. If you test well in math, you rise to the top of that subject. If not, you are left to linger in the middle of the bell curve. The troubling part is that this testing can put you into a box that your school's administrators are comfortable with, even if it is not necessarily right for you.

Education has never been more important, especially when it comes to learning the basics that we all need to survive in today's world. Turning that education into a real advantage relies not only on your teachers, but on your ability to know where your strengths and weaknesses lie, as well as having an understanding of your own interests, likes and dislikes.

You may not be born with the body of an Olympic athlete, but you can still enjoy swimming and running. You may not be born with an ability to run numbers in your sleep, but that does not mean you cannot run a business. Success in life means being aware of those things you are naturally good at and those things you are not. Being good at something does not mean you have to pursue it. Being bad at something does not mean you cannot enjoy it. But in both cases, being aware of your natural ability to do anything will help you set your expectations to the right levels. Being realistic is part of being true to who you are. It is also part of creating a life with which you will be happy.

Personally, I was not born with the body of an Olympic swimmer, nor was I born with the voice of an opera singer, or even a lounge singer for that matter. Neither of those facts means that I cannot enjoy swimming, nor have fun singing. Neither of those facts means I should not work one hundred percent to become the best swimmer or singer I can be. It merely means that those are probably not the areas that I should set Olympic or operatic hopes on if I want to be happy. Instead I should enjoy swimming for swimming's sake. I should enjoy singing as much as I want to. But I should also enjoy the smirk my wife gives me when I belt out an off-key song that I don't remember the words to.

I should embrace my faults as much as my abilities. Because both are a part of whom I am. Both can bring me happiness, but only if I embrace them and learn to live with them, rather than to be frustrated by them.

Throughout your journey, you need to keep in mind that desire and ability are two entirely different things. If you desire something and do not have a natural ability for it, then it can bring you misery and frustration if you set your sights on an unrealistic goal. If you have the ability to be great at something, but no desire, no matter how good you become you will never truly be happy. Only by being realistic about where your desire and your natural ability intersect will you be able to live a life that is both rewarding and fulfilling.

When you reboot your operating system with the Simple Truth you will re-discover yourself based on the life you have lived and the lessons you have learned. You will be able to grow based on your ability to love your faults as well as your perfections. Both are part of the real YOU and you need to embrace them equally if you are to find happiness.

So be aware of your faults. Hold them close to you. Know that they are a part of what makes you, YOU. If you do this, they will no longer limit you, but will augment your journey and even teach you some of what you are here to learn.

Ignore the Influence of Consumerism

There are two conflicting urges that have helped humans evolve to the top of the food chain. One is the need to compete, to be on top. The second is our desire to come together.

The first is a drive that we share with every animal on earth. It caused us to leave the primordial plains and forests in search of better hunting grounds. It drove us to compete with other animals and eventually each other for better resources and habitats. It drove us to create spears and weapons and machines, as well as cures and remedies and technology; all in our drive to survive and to be on top. The second is the desire to come together as a group, a tribe, a family. This urge drove us to work together and to create complex social structures.

They are Ying and Yang in nature. Constantly pushing and pulling us in seemingly different directions, but really moving us forward. At times these urges have banded us together for the common good. They pushed us to create better ways to hunt animals much larger than ourselves. They have driven us to the edge of destruction yet also pulled us back from it. One trait we share with all of the animals on earth. The other lifts us above and sets us apart. One tends to drive us toward our old programming. The other leads us to transcend it.

As a species we are now at a time where our natural tendency toward competition is causing us to undermine our own advances. We no longer need to compete in order to survive.

Instead we compete for ego, for respect and for selfishness rather than survival. It is causing us to drain our natural resources, detrimentally impact our environment, and drive the very species we rely on to extinction. We are pushing ourselves to consume all of the resources just to maintain an unrealistic standard of living, leaving little for the future. The scary thing is that this is not the first time people have destroyed themselves by using up their resources. It is the first time though, that humans are doing this on a global scale.

On a more individual level, every one of us allows our natural tendency to compete and our old programming to undermine ourselves. Advertisers, politicians and brands leverage that primal urge to sell everything from bigger cars and kitchen gadgets to the latest style and the newest mobile devices.

For most of you the act of basic survival is not as much of an issue as it was a thousand years ago. Instead of vying for better hunting grounds and farmland most of us are competing for better jobs and nicer homes. We have turned our competitive programming away from the need to survive and toward the desire for comfort and a position in our society. Today, we compete for status over everything else.

Advertisers are aware of this, and they use your base programming to sell to you. There is a saying in the advertising world that sex and fear are the best ways to sell anything. Is it any wonder? These are the very urges that are so deeply programmed into us. They have kept us growing and evolving as a species: the fear of falling behind, and the urge to propagate the species. The problem arises when these impulses begin to overcome your better sense in today's world.

Your natural inclination to come out on top is used by brands to influence you. They do this by making you feel less than adequate if you don't buy what they are selling. If you don't have the latest mobile device you feel as if you are being left behind. If you don't have the hottest runway style you feel as if you can't compete in the marketplace.

We politely call it consumerism, and it causes you to make decisions that simply are not in your best interest. In today's society you need to feel confident enough in yourself that you don't need to buy what others are selling – just what you truly need or want to buy. If you learn to do this then you set yourself free from one of the most destructive impulses you have – the need to belong at the cost of yourself.

In the last fifty years, the influence of the media has grown exponentially. Where it used to reside on the pages of newspapers and in thirty-second television commercials, it is now everywhere. From outdoor billboards to websites and even cell phones, advertising has become the way for every media outlet to make more money. That means that the brands who want to sell you something have a way to reach you every second of your day with the message of their choice. Rarely is that message to your benefit. It is there to make you feel the need to buy a product regardless of what you, as an individual, need.

Most experts agree every one of you sees close to 3,500 advertising messages every single day. Between advertisements in newspapers and circulars, ads on websites, messaging on cell phones and mobile devices, every one of you is inundated with a reason why you are not good enough unless you buy what they are selling.

Think about your day. How many times do you compare something you own to what someone else owns? How many times have you had a conversation like this rolling in your head?

> I need to get some new shoes. I mean these are fine, but they just don't make me feel good about myself any more. They just don't make me feel special. Those shoes I saw in Vogue looked hot. Maybe I can find a pair before I go out tonight.

Or:

> I really like that new lawnmower I saw in the Home Depot circular. I've got mine, but it's an old model. Besides this one has a drink holder. It's pricy, but come one, I mow the lawn every month. I deserve it.

Your shoes still work. Your old lawnmower still mows the lawn. But inside your head they are just not good enough. The message you have retained is "what will my shoes or my lawnmower say about me to my friends and neighbors? What will people say when I walk out of a room?"

If it's not your shoes or your lawnmower, then it might be your deodorant that you worry about. Perhaps you think that you are not going to feel as confident as you should when you need to most. You worry about what your boss will think when you raise your arms in victory, only to have dark stains under them, or what your date will say when you call for the waiter only to show your stained shirt.

These are not your thoughts, they are the thoughts advertisers have impressed upon you. Now that you no longer live in a prehistoric forest this is how your natural programming is being put to use today. It is being used by advertisers to sell you whatever is in vogue, or whatever they have in stock.

Your own natural tendency to compete and to doubt yourself is why you tune into today's popular television shows. It is why today's ads are so effective in selling everything from cars to perfumes to electronic devices. They make you think to yourself, "I'll never measure up to this person on television that everyone likes. But if I buy this, I may just feel confident enough to hold my head high. Then I too will be a success. I will be able to compete."

Well guess what, no matter what you buy after you have made your purchases, after the thrill of the new product wears off, you will still be exactly who you are. You will be right back where you started from; with yourself. That means being the same person you were at the start, with all the same doubts, the same fears, and the same feeling of being anxious that you had before. You will still be you, and all of that spending will just send you deeper and deeper into a cycle of consumerism. Until you break it yourself.

To free yourself from this cycle you must first learn to be aware of it. You need to learn how you change physically, emotionally and mentally when you see an ad that speaks to you. There is nothing wrong with buying something new. As long as it is something you want, rather than something an advertiser wants you to have.

Once you are aware of how you change then it is up to you to choose how you respond. If you pause before responding, then you have the freedom to change the channel, turn the page, or move to another website. You can buy something different. You can buy what you want and need without sacrificing yourself or your future for it.

If you take yourself out of the message, you will notice that answering the call of advertising is how most people live their lives. For the most part, people respond to advertising as if it were another person. Taking that message at face value and without questioning what they are saying, without really thinking. If you learn to be more aware of an advertiser's messages, you can remove yet another outside level of influence in your life and get one step closer to living the life you love.

So listen to yourself the next time you find yourself drawn to an advertisement. Listen to the way others draw attention to the clothes they wear, be aware of the way they describe what they have on. Are they telling you why they love it? Or, are they repeating the message they received from a salesperson or in an advertisement? You may be surprised at who is really talking.

As important, the next time you see something on sale, or have that "just gotta have it" feeling, learn to separate yourself from your internal message. Stop yourself from responding quickly. Take a breath and pause before you reach for a credit card. Think about what is being pitched and how much you really need whatever is being sold. Stop for a moment and ask yourself out loud, "do I really need this?" "Did I want this two days ago?" "Did I even know it existed two weeks ago?" If not, your desire to buy is probably not your own. It is a reflection of the advertisements you have seen, heard, watched or read. Understand that your internal dialogue is more than likely your own parroting of an advertiser's message.

Break this habit, and you can begin to live the life you want. [6]

Focus Your Unfocused Mind

Two words I repeat quite often in this book are awareness and mindfulness. Don't over-analyze these words. They are not mystical. They are self-describing and simply refer to a state of mind in which you have greater clarity of yourself and the world around you. Both are also essential tools that will help you adjust your own internal programming.

---

[6] Living your life with CaRE, described later in this book, will help you actualize this.

When brought into your life as a daily practice, they will keep you grounded and enable you to manage your life no matter what the world throws at you. These tools will help you start making the right life-choices so that you can stay true to yourself and pursue a more evolved existence. But like any tool, neither awareness nor mindfulness will magically appear. It takes practice and training to be able to focus your unfocused mind.

As you may have guessed at this point, being aware of who you are and how the world influences your life is the first step to evolving. Being aware of yourself and the world will help you manage your life and truly live the life you want to live. As you start down your path to a more evolved you, there will be a constant stream of distractions. By staying focused you can reduce the influence of the people, the advertisers and your own programming that will prevent you from living the life YOU were meant to live. By slowing down the process and limiting the influences of the world around you, you can hit the pause button on your old programming to put YOU back in control.

Like anything in life, you will stumble from time to time. You will find yourself distracted. You will kick yourself more than once for giving in to an ad or a friend's nagging. Don't worry about it. This is natural. This is part of life. But the quicker you can learn to refocus your mind the faster you can get back on track and continue to grow.

Being distracted is a very human trait. It is your old programming at work, the one looking out for things that are out of place that might do you harm. While this trait helped our ancestors' spot dangers lurking in the grass, it now acts to draw you from your own better judgment.

When something is out of order it is human nature to stop what you're doing so that you can put it back in place. When something is broken, your instinct is to fix it. Children do it without even having to learn why. You are simply wired to constantly look for things that are out of place, to fix them and then move on until you find something else that is not quite right.

We have all heard that song on Sesame Street? It goes something like this:

> "One of these things is not like the other; one of these things just doesn't belong..."

This same program is one of the reasons you have such problems maintaining your focus. You lose attention quickly because you are always looking for the next problem to fix. Today, with thousands of bits of information being hurled at you through computers, cell phones, newspapers and magazines, it is no wonder that your basic instincts are now working against you.

When a new task is thrown on your lap your natural response is most likely to smile and accept it. Perhaps you curse a little on the inside, but your instinct is to grin and bear it. How many times have you said to yourself, "I'm not sure exactly how to do this, but let's just get started. We can figure out how to do it along the way."

This is your old programming pushing you forward. It doesn't pause to allow you to think through a problem. More than likely, it causes you to overwhelm yourself before you are even aware that you are juggling more tasks than you can manage. It is now so prevalent we've even given it a name. We now call it "multi-tasking;" as if categorizing our inability to focus makes it alright. When this trait gets out of control we have another term for it. We call it Attention Deficit Disorder, or ADD.

Doctors and scientists recognize that we are incapable of performing two tasks at the same time. Our mind simply cannot process information in that way. When you are multi-tasking what you are really doing is jumping between individual tasks at a faster and faster pace. Most times you end up performing both tasks marginally, which usually gets noticed in the end.

Think about the last time you were multi-tasking. What were you actually doing? When you were writing an email with a phone to your ear, you were not really taking part in the conversation. Instead, you were probably responding in monosyllables, hoping that the other person wouldn't notice. Instead of listening to what they were saying, you were listening for a change in their tone to know when a response was expected. When you finally sent your email, you then turned your attention to the conversation at hand and tried to pick up where you left off. The resulting email probably had errors in it and the person on the other end of the phone probably had a good feeling that you weren't really paying attention.

Instead of trying to do everything at once, start thinking about the concept of "uni-tasking." Simply focusing on the project at hand until it is completed or comes to a stopping point before starting something else. You will be surprised at how much that single focus can accomplish.

Simple Truth

You are far more transparent than you think.

In the same vein, think about how wonderful it would be at the end of the week if you could go home without a list of unfinished projects waiting for you to return to work on Monday. Think about how good it would feel to start the new week without having to pick up the projects you left unfinished from the week before. Or even the month before. That is the difference between focusing your efforts on just a few tasks until they are finished, and forcing your mind to race to whatever the next project happens to be.

Imagine what a difference it would make in your life if you did that for yourself. Instead of going through life jumping at whatever is thrown your way, what if you were able to stop yourself before you jumped and thought about the choice before you? The simple answer is that you could shape your life.

Having a focused mind does not mean becoming a workaholic. It doesn't mean always being "on." It means pausing your thinking so that you can focus your energy on the projects and issues that you want to. It means committing to the task you want to deal with one hundred percent, no matter what that task is. If you want to relax, then relax. But truly relax. If you want to read a book, then read a book. But do it one hundred percent. If you want to watch television then find a show that you really will enjoy and watch it. But do not surf the channels for hours on end in the hopes that a show will come along. Because when you do that, you are simply going back to the comfort of your old programming and the distractions of the world around you.

Living with focus, means living in the moment without distractions. It means being passionate about what you are doing right now, no matter what that is. Instead of relying on your old habits to guide your life, start thinking about what you really want and do it.

Think about this scenario:

> You've had a long day at work. You arrive home exhausted, and what you really want to do is relax and recharge yourself. So you sit in front of the television with a remote in your hand. The show on the screen is a rerun, so you start to flick through the channels hoping to find something good. Two hours later you still

> haven't relaxed, only now you're frustrated that you just wasted your evening with nothing to show for it.
>
> Or:
>
> Or perhaps you sit, half awake at your keyboard, checking email and cruising around on your social networks, hoping to find an interesting conversation. When you finally turn off your computer, it's past midnight and again you're exhausted.

Neither of these distractions allows you to truly relax and recharge. Instead, they are just another mile that you have logged on your own personal treadmill. They are excuses you make for yourself when you let your programming lead your life in today' world.

Ever wonder why you are so comfortable channel surfing? It gives your brain a stream of new material to view without any need to engage in any of it. It is brain candy.

If rest is what you are after, then your television is not the way to go. It is like the empty calories found in a candy bar. It may give you a short burst of what you need, but the feeling is fleeting at best.

If rest is what you are after then put down the remote control and rest. If it is entertainment you are after then wait until you have found an entertaining show before you turn the television on. Otherwise you're just finding an excuse for distraction, rather than living a focused life.

Later in this book you will learn about meditation and other ways to focus your unfocused mind. But for now you should just become, and there is the word again, "aware", of the time you are spending online socializing or watching television.

Start a diary of how much time you spend every evening giving more and more of yourself to the electronic void. Start to realize what you could accomplish if you only spent half of this time reading a book, learning about art, acquiring more skills. This is not about adding more work to your life. It is about focusing your life on the things that truly matter to you. It is about making the most of one of the most precious resources you have – time – and by focusing your energies in a way that supports your own Simple Truth, rather than the distractions of the world.

If you are stressed because of your work, then focus on releasing some of that stress. Take a break or do some exercise so that you can start fresh the next day. Staying late at the office and working at a rapidly declining pace will never help. Believe me, I have tried.

By focusing your mind on whatever it is that you truly want to do, you will find that you actually do have more than enough hours in a day to do the things that mean the most to you. You will simply stop wasting time on projects that have little meaning in your life. Better still, you will find that you will start to accomplish those things that actually have meaning in your life. And every one of those accomplishments will make you feel better about yourself, will help you grow, and will help you accomplish even more.

With focus you will find that you have begun to live a life that is filled with purpose. You will begin to feel the power and energy that comes from living a life that is 100% you, rather than a life diluted by the world around you.

So take the first step by becoming aware of yourself and the world around you. Be aware of how often in the day your mind wanders. Be aware when your emotions get you off track and cause you to lose focus. Don't berate yourself for your lack of focus, just be aware of how your mind wanders during the day.

At the same time, start to be aware of the change in yourself when you become focused on a task. Be aware of how the rest of the world melts away and how even time seems to bend a bit when you simply focus your mind. Then realize what is possible once you learn to focus your mind on what is most important to you.

Exercise – Outside Message Awareness

It is important to always be aware of the real world that you live in. It is equally important to recognize the influences that shape your life. Plan to spend a day building your awareness of the world around you. Learn to expand your awareness beyond what you see before you. Take the time to become aware of the world that exists in the periphery of your life. In this case, the level of advertising that your brain receives even though you may not be conscious of it.

While you might think your brain doesn't recognize this, think again. Your brain is aware of movement, even when you're not focusing on it. You snap your head when you "see" something out of the corner of your eyes. Your head turns when you hear an unfamiliar sound. You jump when you think you feel something on your leg.

Even though your focus is elsewhere, that doesn't mean your brain doesn't recognize and respond to the stimuli that reaches you on a subconscious level. While you may not actively see an advertisement at the periphery of your vision it is still there, your brain still registers it, and you respond by adding stress and pressure to your life on a daily basis.

When you find yourself walking or driving to work in the morning, make a mental note of how many advertising messages you see and hear. Count each billboard and poster you pass, count each banner ad on your computer. Count each brand name on the products that you use or the clothes people wear. When it is safe, turn your head and count all of the advertisements that are on the periphery of your sight.

You don't have to do this for the entire day. Just take a few minutes at different points in your day; when you are commuting to work, when you are on the Internet, when you are at the supermarket. Begin to understand how many messages your subconscious sees daily.

Some of you may live in the country and will not see many. Others may live in a city and will see hundreds before you even leave your home. In either case, you will probably feel inundated, to say the least. And this doesn't even take into account the influence of friends, workmates, and family.

Do this simple exercise from time to time so that you become aware of just how flooded you are with outside input. Start to think about how this outside influence affects your general levels of stress, and how it influences the decisions you make on a subconscious level.

It is important to understand just how much of your life is bombarded by outside influences and messages so that you can start to monitor, and change how your body and mind respond to the world around you. Only then can you begin to transform your life in the way YOU want to.

Step 2: Build YOUR Foundation and Evolve

Know Your State of Mind

Imagine yourself in a doctor's waiting room. Picture yourself bored and leafing through a magazine, barely glancing at the pages. You continue like this not even reading the story in front of you, until the nurse calls out your name.

This is how most people live their lives; going through the motions in a semi-aware state, oblivious of the world around them until a meaningful event stops them in their tracks and wakes them up. It's probably how you might even live a portion of your life.

Now, imagine yourself again in that waiting room. You are still reading your magazine, only this time you find an article that interests you. You stop flipping the pages mindlessly and start to read. You are now conscious of the story in front of you. You are no longer flipping pages in a daze. Your brain becomes active and you focus more of your attention on the article.

As your state of mind changes, so too does your body. You shift in your seat. Perhaps you sit up a little straighter, your pulse quickens just a bit as you become aware of the article in your hands. When your name is called, you may even ask for another minute so that you can get to a stopping point in the article. This is what it is like to be conscious. You are now aware of your thoughts and your body. You start to make choices based on your needs.

Now, imagine the article you're reading is so fascinating that you become absorbed into the concepts and not just the words. As you focus on the story, the events of the waiting room fade into the background. Imagine being so absorbed in your article that you don't even hear the attendant calling out your name. It's not so hard to picture this. It has happened to a lot of you. In many ways, this is what it is like to meditate. It has nothing to do with orange robes or hemp mats. It has nothing to do with incense or burning candles. It has everything to do with your ability to focus your mind on a single idea, so much so that the distractions of your daily life are no longer relevant.

Meditation starts with simply focusing your consciousness. But unlike reading a magazine, it does not have to end when the article is over. Once you learn how to stop the outside world from interrupting your contemplation, you will open up a new world of experiences, a new world of articles that you can explore whenever you want. They will empower your life long after you have put the magazine down.

Let us go back to the example of the waiting room. Imagine you are still reading your article, only this time you come across a profound idea that causes you to close your eyes so that you can spend a few minutes to just think about that idea. You let the idea roll around in your head until the article is no longer important, but the idea is. You turn your focus inward. You find yourself focusing your mind, not on someone else's words, but into your own thoughts. So much so, that you stop trying to learn from the experience of the article, and start to learn from the experiences within your own mind. You simply allow yourself to be a part of the concept behind the article. This is akin to what some call "oneness", the "fourth state", Prajna or Turiya. This is a state of consciousness where truth, self and reality combine. It is a point where you will have truly awakened.

This is an example of the progression through the different states of consciousness. It is similar in many ways to the path you will take as you reboot your old programming. You will start by becoming aware of the world around you, the "waiting room." You will start to explore your own Simple Truth, as if it were an article. As you begin to peel back the layers on yourself, you will undoubtedly start to focus your attention on your own core, so that you can eventually delve into your true self.

Simple Truth

Inhale. Exhale. Enjoy the day.

As with the example, meditation is the key to raising your level of consciousness, and is the best way to explore your own Simple Truth. Forget all the trappings. Meditation is simply a practice that enables you to gain greater awareness of why you are doing what you are doing. When you build your own awareness, you will be able to slow down your actions and even insert a "pause button" on your life, so that you can make the right choices to guide your life in the direction you want it to go. In effect, you can short-circuit the old programming and start to create new patterns to follow.

Meditation is the key to reprogramming yourself. It will give you the balance and the mental strength you need to break through your old habits and programming. It will also give you the ability to change how you react to the world around you and evolve.

But before you learn how to meditate you must learn how to breathe.

Learn to Breathe

One of the most important lessons you can learn from this book is how to simply breathe properly. Breathing is something we all take for granted. Unfortunately most people don't do it correctly and lose out on one of the greatest tools they have for changing their lives.

If you know how to breathe correctly you will find that a deep breath can quickly calm you or it can energize your day. You can ground yourself in a breath and give yourself the stability you need to respond to a situation properly and make the kind of choices that will lead your life in the right direction.

Most people take breathing for granted. It is something you do every day without thinking twice about it. You entered into this life with a crying gasp for air. You will most likely exit it with a final exhale. Between those two breaths you will fill your lungs with fifteen to twenty breaths every minute. This is roughly 21,000 to 29,000 breaths every day. You will take the vast majority of these without thinking. "So how," as one of my clients asked, "can I possibly be breathing wrong? I'm alive aren't I?"

Well, yes and no. Yes, you are alive. But you are probably living your life at a fraction of your potential. Your life is nowhere near where it could be if you simply started to breathe correctly.

The reality is that on just a physical level, you are not getting what your body needs out of every breath. Take just a minute to think about it. While the average lung capacity of an adult male is about 6 liters, the average breath is only about 0.5 liter. With every breath you are not only taking in good oxygen, you are also expelling toxins and poisons like carbon dioxide. With the shallow breath that most people take, the majority of the gases in your lungs that should be exhaled aren't. Even worse, because Carbon Dioxide [O2] is heavier than Oxygen [O], it sits on the bottom of your lungs stagnating. Now, guess where most of the work exchanging bad gases for good gases takes place. That's right, in the bottom third of your lungs, the very part that is filled with the un-exhaled gases.

In the West you are taught to breathe deeply by throwing your shoulders back, expanding your chest and inhaling. It's the picture of the great outdoors we all remember. Unfortunately your ribs are designed to protect your lungs. They are not built to expand to your lung's full capacity.

If you try to take a deep breath just by expanding your ribcage, your ribs will stop you from inhaling fully. Your tendons and muscles will tense up before your lungs get a full intake of oxygen, which will send you into a minor panic. It will actually increase your need for air rather than giving you the full breath your body was looking for.

If this reminds you of your breathing, you are not alone. Most people in the West are shallow breathers who only use the upper portions of their lungs. Imagine what you could do with a full, energizing breath of air twenty times every minute of your day? Imagine the energy you could gain. Imagine the calm you could create for yourself.

If you ever wondered why you stop to take a really deep breath every once in a while, it is because your body is trying to properly exhale the old, stale gases in the bottom of your lungs so that it can fill your lungs with the fresh air you need.

Watch how a baby breathes. They breathe from their bellies. They draw their diaphragm down and pull air into their lungs, expanding them fully. When they exhale, they do so by compressing the diaphragm and releasing the carbon dioxide fully. It is easy and natural, without adding any stress on their bodies and without moving their ribs.

If you can relearn to breathe this way, you will have one of the greatest tools you can imagine for instantly reducing your stress, for staying calm and for taking control of your life. Yes it may give you a bit of a Buddha belly for a minute, but really, for all that you gain you cannot be that vain. Or can you?

If you think this is a lesson to pass over, don't. Studies have linked focused breathing with reducing hot flashes in menopausal women, relieving chronic pain and reducing symptoms of PMS. Some hospitals have even begun teaching relaxation breathing to patients to treat them for a wide range of conditions. In fact while recovering from my surgeries, the doctors always put me on a daily breathing exercise to ensure I was breathing deeply and that I did not leave stagnant air in my lungs – one of the primary causes for infections in hospital patients.

Years ago I was fortunate to learn how to breathe properly in my martial arts training. My instructors taught me to breathe into my belly. It was a way to stay grounded during my workouts and helped maintain my center and my focus. After my surgeries I found myself coming back to my breathing as I lay in bed. It helped me to focus on my healing, and afterwards on my life.

I found myself taking a few deep, cleansing breathes as I lay in bed. It also helped me to manage some of the more shocking news that was given to me. It enabled me to hit an emotional pause button and stopped me from making the kind of automatic responses that rarely eased my stress. And yes, that was part of the beginning to learning the secret behind the Simple Truth. You can start to do the same by learning how to take a simple breath.

Pay Attention to Your Breath

As I mentioned before, one of the reasons we breathe at all is to cleanse the body. With every breath you get rid of old and stale gases and exchange them for fresh oxygen. With every inhale you bring in fresh oxygen, nutrients, and vital energy. With every exhale you expel carbon dioxide and other toxins and poisons that your body produces. Think of this the next time you take a breath. It will help you understand what it takes to keep your body going and place greater attention on what it takes to feel alive.

The first step to proper breathing is through what is called **Attention Breathing**. As its name implies it focuses your attention on the natural rhythm of your breath. When you practice this do not try to control your breathing, simply pay attention to it. Just observe it. Learn to be aware of your breathing so that you can shift from the unconscious breathing you are used to, to conscious breathing.

Lie down with one hand on your stomach and the other on your chest. Now draw your diaphragm down to your waist and feel your stomach expand. Do this slowly so that you are taking deep, relaxed breaths. Only the hand on your stomach should move, it should rise and fall slowly as you inhale and exhale. The hand on your chest should remain motionless. Take as long as you comfortably can with each breath. Don't worry about counting or timing yourself. Just feel the air coming into your lungs and moving your stomach outward.

Practice doing this at several points during your day. Take a few minutes to just concentrate on how it feels to breathe. Become attuned to how your body feels with each breath. Feel the air as it enters your nostrils and tickles the hairs in your nose. Follow your breath downward as it flows into your lungs. Feel your diaphragm expand downward and outward, and notice how deeply your breath reaches into your belly. Do not exhale immediately, but keep the air in your lungs for a few seconds. Allow your body to exchange the toxins. Now exhale and feel them leave your body. As you exhale focus on the air leaving your lungs, out your windpipe and through your nostrils. You can even turn the edges of your mouth upward into a small smile as you do this – but that is completely voluntary.

Do not try to change the natural pace of your breath. Just become aware of how you feel as you breathe. All you should be doing is observing your breath now that you are breathing properly. You may start to feel more relaxed. You may even become light-headed, or get a little dizzy. That is fine. Stop if you feel uncomfortable. At first you may only do this for a few minutes. As you get used to how your body responds, you can increase the time you take to breathe in this way.

Now that you know how to breathe properly, you may even think about taking a few minutes to breathe just before going to bed to relax you. Or, perhaps you can do this as you wake up to ease you into your day. You may even want to take a few minutes out of a stressful workday to refresh yourself with a few deep breaths.

Without even thinking about it, you will find that your body will naturally tend to breathe properly because it likes what it is feeling.

The Complete Healthy Breath

Once you have gotten used to breathing into your diaphragm, take it one step further with what is called a Complete Healthy Breath.

Most people think there are two parts to every breath – an inhale and an exhale. There are actually three. Simply inhaling and exhaling doesn't give the lungs very much time to exchange and purge the body of the harmful gasses and toxins that it is trying to expel with every exhale.

To take a Complete Healthy Breath, simply insert a pause between each inhalation and exhalation. It only needs to be for a second or two to slow down the breath and allow your body to process the fresh oxygen while expelling even more harmful toxins. Technically, this creates four separate actions for each breath: Inhalation, Retention, Exhalation, and Suspension.

You are not holding your breath you are simply pausing for a second or two and slowing down your breathing to allow your body to catch up. Start to do this during your workday. Take a few minutes when you are stressed to relax yourself or when you are falling asleep during a meeting to energize yourself. You will find that your body will balance itself for the situation at hand. But you have to give it the breath it needs to do so.

You will be amazed at how something as simple as proper breathing can have such a profound effect. And yes, if you have not guessed it by now, the simple practice of a Complete Healthy Breath will naturally take you into meditation. But before we go there, let's look at some other forms of breathing that will be useful to you.

The Cleansing Breath

The **Cleansing Breath** is not a casual breath. It is a way to deepen and expand proper breathing to better expel the toxins and re-energize yourself.[7] With a Cleansing Breath you will breathe deeper and exhale more fully, so you may want to practice this sitting or lying down in case you become a little dizzy. And no, this should not be done while driving or operating heavy machinery.

Like a Complete Healthy Breath, a Cleansing Breath breaks each breath into four distinct parts. Again, this maximizes oxygen intake and enables your body to move the oxygen-rich blood throughout your body. The deeper breaths also clean and invigorate the lungs, increasing their capacity over time and increasing your energy and well-being.

With each breath, fill the lungs from the bottom up. Give them time to exchange all of the old gases and toxins completely before you expel the air into the sky.

Inhale
Inhale through your nose by expanding your diaphragm downward and pushing your abdomen down and out. Feel your stomach expand as you bring air inward. Once your abdomen is full, continue inhaling and expand the chest, filling the upper lungs. Raise your collarbone and your chest upward while pulling the shoulder blades back to bring in even more air. Continue to inhale as you fill your throat and nose, topping off your breath. You can even throw your arms back and make your body as large as possible.

---

7 If you are a smoker or are suffering from asthma, or have other respiratory illnesses consult a doctor before attempting this. Be careful and don't over-exert yourself.

Retain
Hold your breath in for up to eight seconds and focus your attention on how full your body feels. Feel your body as it circulates the newly enriched blood and feel your muscles respond.

Exhale
Slowly exhale through your mouth by pushing your abdomen up and in. Keep exhaling to push the air from the lungs and contract your ribs. You may find yourself slumping forward as you do this. That is okay. Exhale all of the air from your lungs, throat, nose and mouth.

Suspend
Hold the breath out until you start to feel discomfort, but for no more than eight seconds. Focus your attention on the emptiness of your lungs. Pause to think about not panicking and gasping for air. Instead draw in a new breath slowly and smoothly. You should not wait until the last second to breathe in. Instead work on establishing a comfortable rhythm so that there is no discomfort.

Repeat
Slowly inhale just as before. Start by bringing air into the bottom of your lungs through your abdomen and filling it with clean oxygen. Feel the sensation of your body filling up again. Focus on how your body feels as it is filled with fresh air.

This is a practice you should try to do several times a week for three to ten breaths. You may find that doing this during the afternoon re-invigorates you for the remainder of the day. In time, you may even want to do this while taking a walk outside of your office to give yourself a much needed break.

There are other breathing techniques that you can learn. But these basic exercises are enough to start with for now.

Develop Your Meditation Practice

The natural extension to proper breathing is of course meditation. As one student said, “this is just like breathing but with focus.” In many ways it is. At this point, there should be little mystery as to why meditation is such an important part of your own evolution. The immediate benefits to meditation are shown in innumerable studies. It is now a practice that is used by leading universities and executive coaches, as well as competitive sports professionals.

Studies show that individuals who meditate quickly reduce stress, are better able to manage their lives and show improvement in both their health and their well being. Groups who meditate have lower crime rates and are generally more productive. In the short-term people who meditate consistently become calmer and are less affected by stress. In the longer term, they are able to make clearer decisions and remove themselves from the kind of rash reactions that people are plagued with in today’s world. Both of these are key elements to your own personal evolution and to living your own life. Even without this, there are so many positive studies associated with meditation that it is hard to understand why more people do not undertake this simple practice.

The Power of Meditation

A great study into the power of meditation occurred in 1986 after the owner of a Detroit based chemical plant instituted transcendental meditation with fifty-two of the company’s one hundred workers – ranging from management to employees working the line. A program was implemented where employees meditated for twenty minutes before coming to work and twenty minutes in the afternoon. They did this on company time and the owner, R.W. Montgomery, saw almost instant results.

In three months, employees stated they had more energy and were able to handle stress better. They also had fewer physical complaints and lower cholesterol levels. Over the next three years it was confirmed that:

- Absenteeism fell by 85%
- Productivity rose 120%
- Injuries dropped 70%
- Profits increased 520%

Since 1930, there have been over 1500 separate studies that are related to meditation and its effects on its practitioners. And these are just the ones that were fully completed. Some statistics on people who meditate include results like:

- A decrease in heart rate, respiration, blood pressure and oxygen consumption.
- A reduced feeling of anxiousness and nervousness, with a greater feeling of independence and self-confidence.
- 75% of people suffering from insomnia were able to fall asleep within twenty minutes of going to bed after starting a daily meditation program.
- Women with PMS showed an improvement in their symptoms after 5 months of daily reflection and meditation.
- A decrease in the thickness of the artery walls which effectively lowers the risk of heart attack or stroke.
- 60% of anxiety prone people showed marked improvements in their anxiety levels after 6-9 months of daily meditation.

For me, one of the most striking benefits of meditating was the reduction of stress and the ability to find greater balance in my own life. Stress is a major cause of many ailments from heart disease and heart failure, to diabetes, high blood pressure and even cancer. In fact, statistics from health insurance companies show that people who meditate on a regular basis are less prone to illness, and can reduce the likelihood of being hospitalized for coronary disease by up to 87 percent. They even go further to say that regular meditation reduces the chance of getting cancer by 55 percent.

So, you might ask, what is the down side? The world has yet to find any.

In my own life, regular meditation has enabled me to start the process of reprogramming myself. It has helped me to live a happier, more productive life. It can do the same for you.

Meditation in Practice – Simple Repetition

To start meditating you do not need to join a monastery or buy new age crystals. You do not need to renounce your faith or give away your earthly possessions. You do not even need to quit your job. If anything, daily meditation will enable you to focus more intently, give you more time in your day, and reduce the distractions that plague everyone. I know what many of you are thinking, but get those thoughts out of your head. There is nothing mystical about meditation and no, it will not change your fashion sensibilities. After all, it's just breathing with focus.

All you need to do is find a quiet place and set aside a few minutes at the start of each day. It can be as little as three. That is it. In time you'll sit for longer periods, but start with just a few minutes and see what happens.

Once you become practiced you will find the benefits of meditation will work their way into every aspect of your life on your own. When you are walking, when you find yourself in a stressful situation, before giving a presentation, or even on your way to your boss's office, you will began to notice greater control over yourself, more balanced thinking, and a much greater awareness of your actions. These are the benefits of meditation that you will begin to see throughout your daily life.

> ***Simple Truth***
>
> *Meditation and mindfulness don't take time, they give time.*

Just realize that meditation is not a one-time fix. It is an ongoing practice that will grow with you and forever improve your life. As you learn more about it, you will find new ways to go deeper and further than you thought possible. You will find greater insight and gain greater awareness into yourself. You will be able to refine your practice so that it supports your needs and your own Simple Truth.

To start, you should use a bit of discipline to get the most out of it. So set aside both a regular time and place to reduce the outside distractions of the world. Make it a bit of "me time" in your day. As your practice grows, you can expand this to half an hour, an hour, or more. But start small. What you do not want to do is set your expectations too high or be too aggressive. More likely than not, that will only lead to frustration. Meditation is a practice where it is more important to start slowly and grow at your own pace. Meditation and the ability to focus may seem simple at first, but they require greater concentration than you might expect.

Find a Quiet Time & Secluded Place

You do not need a personal chapel or a private alter to start meditating. All you need is enough space to sit with your legs crossed. If this is uncomfortable, you can prop yourself up by sitting on a firm pillow, or you can purchase a meditation pillow just for this. Do not trade off austerity at the cost of comfort. You want to be able to focus on your own mind, not on the cramps that will come from being uncomfortable.

Your space should be out of the way and somewhat secluded from interruption. It should be one that you are comfortable in and that you can return to. But really this can be anywhere. What you want is a place that your mind and body can begin to recognize as a place of escape, a sanctuary, which will help to speed a deeper meditation. You may need to remove extraneous clutter from the area so that there are fewer distractions. After all, cleanliness is... well, you know the rest.

As your experience grows you will find yourself meditating during a flight, on the train, before a meeting. What I have found, and as one of my Sensei's recommended, the best time to meditate is early in the morning before your day begins.

That means before your husband, wife or partner rises and before your children wake. In the beginning allow ten to twenty minutes for yourself. But even two or three minutes is enough. It will be frustrating at first. You will also wonder when your great breakthrough is going to happen. It will come when you are ready for it. Until then, you will see smaller changes happen. You will also learn to value the time that you dedicate to it as you grow to enjoy it more and more.

Maintain a Peaceful Atmosphere

Once you have found a peaceful time and place for your daily meditation, make sure that you maintain the feeling of calm and quiet throughout your time there. This is important to your meditation. You want to train your mind and body to associate your space with a feeling of calm and relaxation. Outside interruptions will only undermine your efforts. It may mean telling your husband, wife or partner that this is your time. It may mean turning off your cell phone so that you are not disturbed. You may also want to turn down the lights or pull the shades to make sure the few minutes you are giving yourself are truly yours. Your goal, especially in the beginning, is to find a place that removes as many distractions as possible, and to that gives you a sense of tranquility so that you can focus on your mind rather than on the world around you.

Simple Truth

Outward growth requires inward exploration.

Be Comfortable

Comfort means many things to many people. Start by wearing comfortable clothing. Loose fitting pajamas, a robe, even boxers or nothing at all is fine. It doesn't matter what you wear, what matters is that they don't bind. Also, refrain from drinking coffee, tea or soda before you meditate. They tend to make you overly active or can give you gas. You may want to stretch a bit before you sit. Loosening up the body prevents you from being distracted by aches or cramps. After all, one of the reasons yoga was created was to prepare the body for long periods of meditation.

I prefer an austere environment, but don't hesitate to place items that help you relax in your meditation space. Props are not required, but yoga mats or cushions can be great for meditation. To put it simply, if your legs are in pain you are not going to be able to focus on your meditation. So make sure you are comfortable to start.

Some people like to have the sound of running water to create a soothing atmosphere. If you want to light the room with a few candles that is fine. As you deepen your practice you will most likely find that less is more. Just remember this should be easy and ongoing. So, to start, it is more important that you set a mood that you will return to time and again.

Assume a Comfortably Formal Pose

As with your clothing, your pose should be comfortable. Do not force your feet or legs into a place they don't want to go. Start by sitting with your legs crossed and a straight back. You can sit on the floor, on a supportive pillow. If you are not comfortable, sitting in a chair is fine.

Next tuck your tailbone forward to straighten out your spine. If you are using a pillow or a chair, move to the front of it so that only your tailbone is supported. Now, straighten your spine as if you are hanging from a string that is attached to the top of your head rather than sitting. Place your hand on your knees creating small circles with your thumbs and middle fingers. Or hold them in your lap, just below your navel making a circle of your fingers and thumbs to remind you of the circle of energy you are a part of.

Finally, raise the outsides of your lips and place a small smile on your face. With it, remind yourself that this should always be a pleasant practice of lightness.

Breathe + Count

Now, close your eyes and breathe into your stomach just as you learned in the last section. At first take several deep breaths through your nose by pulling your diaphragm downward. Your chest and ribs should not move at all. Only your stomach should move. Fill your lungs completely until your stomach is fully extended, then hold the air in your lungs for a moment. Finally, exhale through your nose, slowly but fully. Pause before your next breath then take another slow and deep breath.

These breaths will help to relax you. They will also help to clear out all the unused air in your lungs. It may cause you to cough or even give you a momentary light-headedness, this is expected. If you become unsettled, open your eyes, refocus yourself, and start your meditation anew.

Now, with your eyes closed, fill your lungs slowly as you count to eight, again through your nose, only using your diaphragm to draw the air in. Let the air circulate in your lungs for a count of two, then exhale slowly for a count of eight through your nose. As you breathe focus on the air passing by the tip of your nose.[8]

Allow your mind to feel your breath enter, circulate around your lungs and then leave your body. If you get distracted, and you will, return to your eight-count. It will help you return again and again to your breath.

When you start your mind will wander. Don't be frustrated by this. It is perfectly natural. If something distracts you, just return to your count of eight-two-eight. As your practice develops you will be able to go for longer and longer periods

[8] Most meditation practices have you focus on three points of breath: the tip of your nose, the rise and fall of your stomach, the entire movement of air through your system.

without your daily life distracting you. You will also start to go deeper and deeper into your own consciousness and that of the greater universe around you.

Time

Time should not be a factor in your meditation practice. Nor should it be used as a way to gauge how well or how deeply your practice is developing. How well you can focus and manage your distractions is. How deeply you can go into your meditation should be. Yet, many people I know use time as a way to track their practice. It's simply an easy way to monitor progress.

At the start, you may only be able to meditate two, three or five minutes. You may come out and look at your watch amazed at how short you were under. This is fine. If you want to set benchmarks, then start meditating for as long as you can. If it's only a few minutes before you have to open your eyes, then simply take a breath, close your eyes and count your breathing for another couple of minutes.

Ideally, in the early stages, aim for ten minutes at a sitting. In today's hectic world, ten minutes may be all you can afford in the morning. But that is still enough time for you to gain some real benefit from it. Also, plan to practice your meditation for three to five times a week. An ideal number would be ten minutes, five days a week. But we all know the realities of life.

After three months of practice, you may want to aim for fifteen or twenty minutes as a goal, three to five times a week. Those that want to deepen your practice should aim for twenty to thirty minutes, three to five times a week. Those that want to maintain a light practice should aim for ten to twenty minutes, three to five times a week.

There really is no right or wrong in terms of meditation – it truly is what is right for you.

Distractions

In the beginning you will find a lot of distractions occur. Your legs will cramp. Your back will slump. Your shoulders will become tense. Simply acknowledge these distractions and reposition your body. Then return to your eight count. If you find yourself twisting, acknowledge it, reposition yourself, and return to your count. If you find your shoulders hunched up, acknowledge it, relax your shoulders, smile and return to your count. If you find yourself drifting off to sleep, acknowledge it, smile, open your eyes if you have to, but return to your count and your meditation. As your body becomes more and more used to sitting for longer periods of time, these distractions will go away.

Just like physical distractions, when you start to meditate thoughts will enter your mind. These are natural. This is your mind clearing itself of issues and events that are plaguing it. Your natural tendency will be to dwell on them. Don't. Instead, simply acknowledge them, smile to yourself and let them go.

I sometimes softly say the word "thoughts" to myself when they arise. It allows me to give each of them a simple nod, before letting them float past. I often imagine them as a cloud that harmlessly dissipates around me as it floats past. Each of these is just a mental tool that allows me to be aware of them without losing my focus.

It Does Not Happen Overnight

At first you may only be able to meditate for several minutes at a sitting. That is fine. Scientists can see physical changes in the brain with only minimal time spent meditating. The only requirement is that you continue to practice. It is better to practice five times a week for a few minutes a day, then to practice once a week for twenty minutes. As your practice grows the time of your meditations will increase, the amount of distractions will decrease, and your ability to focus will deepen.

Be comfortable in the idea that meditation is not a one-time quick fix. It is an ongoing practice. As you begin you will undoubtedly have frustrations. You will also experience subtle transformations as well as some amazing breakthroughs.

You can sit for hours on end meditating day after day without seeing much of a difference in yourself. Then, one day, after closing your eyes and breathing you will find yourself in a place that you have never been before. You will experience the kind of serenity that you have probably only dreamed of.

Meditation can be like climbing up a series of plateaus, where each plateau gives your mind a place to rest with the knowledge that there are more levels to reach just ahead. Each plateau will give you a better sense of well being and self control. But each also requires more focus and work to get to the next.

One of the most striking elements to meditation is how your practice will seep into the rest of your life. You will find yourself walking down the street seeing the world with a level of clarity that you never had before. You will find yourself completely aware of your surroundings, but able to remain separate from them. You will notice that you are able to process everything as it happens, but without a sense of panic or the need to immediately respond. You may even find yourself in a meeting, watching, observing, and having the wherewithal to insert yourself where you want to, again, without the panic of failure you may have had in the past.

For me and thousands of others meditation can take away the anxiety we all feel while giving you the ability to maintain a sense of harmony no matter what the world throws at you. This is why it is such a crucial part to defining a new you and reprogramming your life. It will give you the ability to distance yourself from the issues that have prevented you from being YOU.

Types of Meditation

Meditation is a great tool to raise your awareness and evolve the way you interact with the world around you. It can also be a great practice to draw upon when you find yourself feeling overwhelmed and on the verge of spinning out of control.

The practice I prefer is generally called Mindfulness Meditation. Yet I have found even this practice has many forms within it. While each of the meditations that follow is designed for a different purpose, they all return to a very basic principle; focus on your breathing.

As you become more comfortable with your meditation, you will find you may even add your own nuance to these styles. You may find you no longer need to count, and can reduce your practice to focusing on your breath or a simple mantra.[9] Or you

[9] I vary between a formal mindfulness meditation or a Zen meditation. However, these are far from the only types of meditation to practice. Have fun. Explore different practices and schools to find one that best suits your needs and personality.

may find that you can sit for longer and longer periods. Regardless of how you make these practices your own you will find that proper breathing and meditation will enable you to employ Mindfulness to remain true to your own Simple Truth. You will also live your life with greater control over your actions and in a happier, more balanced manner.

You will find that there are endless variations to the basic practice of meditation. For those who are highly agitated, meditating to music can provide enough background noise to still the mind. For those that are restless, there is walking meditation to provide a physical release. There is yoga and the traditional martial arts that are deeply based in breathing and meditation. You may want to explore some of the different forms of meditation once you have started your practice and developed a basic appreciation for what is generally known as mindfulness meditation.

Connection Meditation

This is a simple meditation that I use to stay centered, especially when the world around me seems to be spinning out of control. I simply look at whatever object is in front of me – a desk, a building, a cloud, a stream – and I start to mentally walk through all the ways it is connected to my life, as well as the ways in which it creates a connection to the world around me. It helps to remind me that this really is a small world, and we are truly interdependent in everything we do.

For instance, I might look at the desk in my office. I use this desk every day. It keeps my tools and my materials at hand. It also gives me a surface to write on and a place from which to reach out to others. It gives me a focal point for my work that keeps me grounded.

Craftspeople built this desk from wood hewn from a tree. All of those people had parents that raised them and fed them. They learned their trade from someone who was likewise raised and fed by others. They all have families that rely on my desk for their income from which they are fed and sheltered. They were all schooled, or are being schooled, with other children who are taught by teachers, who each have families they care for. The craftspeople and teachers were all fed with food grown on a farm. That farm was fertilized by fishmeal cast off from fishermen and sold through a network of men, women and businesses. Each of those men and women has families that they work to take care of.

The tree that provided the wood for the desk took energy from the same sun I see outside my window. It was watered by a stream. That stream was filled by rain that evaporated from a lake thousands of miles to the West. Its roots fed on the nutrients left by a squirrel that had passed on.

The connections and interconnections are endless. The important part is not how many you can find, but that you see how interdependent we are, how the network of life is an endless circle that eventually comes back to you. But most important, this simple meditation grounds me by reminding me how life itself is a miracle to enjoy.

Walking Meditation

In many ways walking meditation is a blend of concentration and mindfulness meditations. It allows you to stand up and bring your meditative mind and practice wherever you go. As with mindfulness meditation, it is essential to maintain your focus on the experience of walking. It is a wonderful way to spend twenty minutes or entire hours getting some exercise while cleansing your mind. It is also an incredible practice to turn a lunch hour into a personal escape.

Before you begin your walking meditation, I recommend starting on a familiar route. A path you have hiked in the woods or a familiar park is a good place to start, as is a beach, a museum, or even a library. Reducing the outside influence allows you to build up your ability to focus and concentrate while you walk.

Start by simply standing and focusing your attention on the ground between your feet. Take a deep, cleansing breath and become aware of your weight on the soles of your feet. Become aware of your weight and your attachment to the earth beneath you. Now, gently rock back and forth, feeling the shift in weight from the balls of your feet to your heels. You do not have to move much. Just be aware of the subtle movements that your body instinctively does to keep you balanced. Realize how many years it took you to learn how to simply maintain your balance.

When you are ready, take a step forward. Do it in time to your breathing. It should be slow and unhurried. Give yourself a few seconds with each step to focus on the sensations as your feet touch and leave the earth. Do not change the way you walk, just be aware of your body as you raise your leg, move your foot forward, and then place it back on the earth.

Focus your attention on the soles of your feet as they make contact with, and then lift from, the ground. With each step you should be aware of the different sensations you experience. Feel your heel touch the ground. Then feel your arch as it presses into the earth or the soles of your shoes. Feel your toes as they grip the ground below you and then push off as you step forward. Be aware of the weight that gravity creates.

Keep your gaze just in front of your feet and watch the ground so that you place your feet exactly where you want them to be placed. As you walk move your attention up your legs. Feel your ankles bend and flex, front and back, but also side to side. Feel your calves stretch and compress with every step. Become aware of your core and how your muscles and spine move. Notice how even your chest and neck adjust to maintain your posture.

Do not force yourself into a posture you are uncomfortable with. Stay relaxed. Keep a smile on your face and in your thoughts so that you radiate confidence with every step. Enjoy yourself as you step forward. Notice if your shoulders are tense or your jaw is tight. Relax both as you keep a soft focus on the world around you. Broaden your horizon so that you take in your path, but also notice the people who pass you, the sky and the clouds, even the rain if it is falling. Remain conscious of the world around you while you remain centered within yourself.

As with sitting meditation, you will become aware of feelings, thoughts and distractions. Acknowledge them, let them pass, and return your focus to the ground just in front of your feet and to your body. Notice the objects around you with a smile but without getting distracted by them.

When you have completed your walk, just come to a natural stop. Stand where you have stopped for a few moments and reflect on your feet and your body. Move your focus slowly up your body paying attention to your legs, your thighs, your abdomen, your chest and your head. Take a moment to reflect on the distractions that you passed by. Realize that you did not have to stop for any of them. Know that they were there, but were in a different world than what you were walking through. Understand that there are two different worlds – your inner world that is affected by your own thoughts, and the world you are living in and walking through.

Most important, understand that you have control over which world you want to be a part of merely by shifting your focus.

Stretching Meditation

Meditation is a great tool to raise your awareness and better manage your interactions with the world around you. It can also be a great practice to draw upon when you find yourself in a stressful situation when you are not sure where to turn.

The next time you find yourself losing control of your emotions, take a mental step back from the situation you are in and give yourself a break, even if for just a few minutes. Instead of jumping into action that you may regret, try the following exercise to ground yourself. Remember meditation is not just a sometime practice. It is a tool that can be done anywhere and anytime you need it.

First, pick a point in front of you that you can focus on. Raise the outer points of your lips so that you have a small smile on your lips. Now, take a deep breath. Forget about what is going on around you as you turn your focus to your breath coming slowly and evenly into your stomach. Feel your breath leaving you. Breathe in again. This time as you exhale, extend your fingers as far as they will go. Really stretch them and feel the energy you're holding in, shoot out through your fingers.

If you need to, close your eyes for a few seconds as you continue to breathe in and out and expel the energy and tension in your body. Feel your body relax. If you sense tension in your shoulders, pull them up to your ears and push them back down to release it. If your neck is tense, roll your head in a slow circle around you. If your back is tense, slowly roll your spine to rid yourself of it.

If your eyes are closed, refocus on the object in front of you. Keep the smile on your face and focus on the muscles that are keeping your lips turned upward. Be conscious of feeling more relaxed and more present in the moment as you respond to your situation.

Before you go back to your day, take a moment to be aware of your feeling relaxed and refreshed. Shrug your shoulders and shake your head to start your transition. As important, be aware of how differently you will respond to people and situations after your meditative break, now that you are less tired and stressed.

Body Awareness Meditation

This is a more active form of meditation that has become a central practice in my day. I use it to increase my awareness of my own thoughts and to provide a greater sense of myself. I also use it to rid myself of anxiousness and create a feeling of calm in myself and in the world around me. It is also a nice way to remind myself of what it takes to do anything in life.

It is also a practice that is now being used by psychologists and therapists as a way to reduce and even alleviate a range of mental and physical conditions such as obsessive-compulsive disorders and in the treatment of depression and drug addiction.

This is not a seated meditation, nor does it focus your attention on a single object like your breath or a mantra. Instead, every aspect of your experience is welcomed and appreciated.

I start by taking a few cleansing breaths. Then I calmly and slowly label everything that I do. In doing this I become aware of my actions and of how complicated and miraculous even a simple task truly is. It creates a greater sense of self and helps me to understand the basic truth of who I am. It also gives me a full appreciation of how much the brain does, even when we do not feel like we are actively engaging it.

With body Awareness Meditation, take the role of an impartial observer of everything that occurs in whatever action you are focusing on. Do not focus on a particular single action like breathing. Instead, work with a larger task, such as eating or washing dishes.

Follow your actions and become mindful and fully aware of what is happening in the present moment. Like other forms of meditation use your breath as a platform from which to start. As you breathe, repeat the word "inhaling, exhaling, inhaling, exhaling," to yourself slowly and evenly. Do not focus on your breath, but just be aware of the fact that you are breathing. Feel your lungs fill and empty. As a thought enters your consciousness, do not judge or comment on it. Instead acknowledge the fact that you have a thought. You can even label is quietly with the word "thinking." Again, the goal is not to focus on the specific thought you are having, but to be aware that you are, in fact, thinking.

As you start with your task, take note of the actions you are doing. If you are cleaning dishes, instead of simply wiping off a dish or running it under the faucet become aware of your actions.

> As you reach for a dish, repeat to yourself "reaching, reaching, reaching"
>
> As you turn a faucet on, repeat to yourself, "turning, turning, turning"
>
> As you wipe a dish, repeat to yourself "wiping, wiping, wiping"
>
> As you dry a dish, repeat to yourself "drying, drying, drying"

Once you are comfortable you can become more detailed in your observations. You can become mindful of your fingers grabbing, touching, and gripping a plate. You can notice sensations of hot water and cold water. If you are eating you can break down the act of eating into grinding, tasting, swallowing.

As you do this you will become aware of how complex even the most simple tasks are. You will also have a greater appreciation of how complex and wonderful a creature you are. Something you may forget when you only look at the world around you without recognizing all the interactions you have with it.

Living Mindfully

Living mindfully is simply a way to bring your meditation practice into your everyday life. Living mindfully means living in a state of purposeful awareness of yourself, of your actions and of the world around you. It is the ongoing act of living in the moment, of observing and responding to the present moment, rather than spending your time worrying about the past or trying to anticipate the future.

> ***Simple Truth***
>
> *Don't try to live your entire day mindfully. Start with small moments. They will come together on their own.*

What makes mindfulness different than merely floating through your day in a daze is the purposefulness and focus that you place on your actions. By being aware that you are being mindful you will take ownership over your actions, and responsibility for the effect they have. This will help you consciously avoid the distractions of the world around you. It will also provide a foundation for your personal evolution.

Just as breathing led to meditation, meditation will lead to mindfulness almost without effort. They are all natural extensions of each other that ebb and flow with your own growth. Each represents a plateau that you can build upon and grow from. Alone, each of these will improve your life. Together, they will give you the tools you need to grow so that you can discover and live your own Simple Truth.

In one sense mindfulness brings your meditation into all aspects of your life. Eating, doing dishes, even waiting for friends can become mindfulness practices. As you explore your actions more closely and learn to observe your own actions, you will find that it brings a quality that resonates throughout your life.

Start your practice by paying greater attention to yourself and the world around you during your day. When you find yourself drifting off, simply stop yourself and center yourself in the present moment. As this act becomes more natural to you, you will find that you will simply start to live your life and a greater sense of what you are doing will permeate your life. At this point you will find that you are able to pause what you are doing so that you can contemplate your choices before you make them, and guide your actions so that they support your goals in living the life you want to live.

Like all things, being able to live mindfully does not happen overnight. It is the result of a constant effort of realization and awareness. Living mindfully means you are aware and conscious of your actions. It also means that you will have greater control over the little choices you are making so that you can start to make the right ones while stopping your old habits and patterns from running your life. You can stop living your life based on your old programming and evolve to the next level simply by making the right choices along the way.

I will go into the "how" behind living mindfully later in this book, but for now understand that everything you are learning will keep taking you higher. Each step you take will build upon what you have already learned, and will lead you to a new plateau for your next step.

Live With CaRE

Every day your life is a never-ending process of responding to the world around you. Every time that you do, your life is thrown into a simple process of Cause and Effect. Regardless of what you are doing, some event will cause a change in your life that you must respond to. For example, let's say someone spills a glass of wine at a party. From that one simple event, a domino effect takes over. One potential outcome is that the glass of wine is spilled and you get doused with red wine which stains your blouse. Another outcome is that the glass of wine is spilled and you move out of the way, preventing a disaster.

Because everyone reacts differently, every series of events is different, so there is never a definitive outcome for a given action. Sometimes the wine misses everyone altogether. At other times people anticipate the glass being knocked over and catch it before any wine is spilled. Some people move quickly, avoiding getting splashed. While others do not respond until after the wine is spilled and their blouse is stained.

As with most events, the longer you wait to respond to a given situation the less control you have in your life and the more you are forced to live with the consequences of someone else's actions. Your ability to **R**espond to an event is the R in CaRE. It is the action you take that creates the **E**ffect you must eventually live with.

If you live mindfully and in a state of awareness of the world around you, you can change how your life unfolds by directing the small choices you make on a daily basis, rather than enabling someone else to make choices for you. This is where living mindfully and mindfulness meditation become such powerful tools. They give you the self control and the ability to pause your decision making process so that you can positively affect the outcome of your life.

CaRE stands for the **Ca**use, **R**esponse, and **E**ffect of every event. It also stands for the **a**ction you can take to create the change you want to create in your life. It means that rather than being forced into the position of an inactive bystander in your own life, you can take action and exert control over how your life unfolds. As versus the Cause and Effect world that our ancestors lived in, you have the ability to exert control over your life. In between the **Ca**use of an event and its **E**ffect on your life, is your ability to **a**ct so that you are not **R**esponding by rote.

Let's face it. Life happens. Events occur. The difference between living through life like you have been and living mindfully, is that by living mindfully you control how you respond to the events around you without being dragged down into them. You can pause your automatic programming so that you can choose how you respond, so that you can make the little choices that will empower you to live the life you want to live. And that makes all the difference.

Let's look at a more common example. You come home from a long day at work exhausted [Cause]. Because you are tired, all you want to do is to sit down and vegetate in front of the television for a while [Response]. However, after just a few minutes of television you become frustrated because nothing that you like is on [Effect]. Yet instead of turning the television off [Cause], you keep watching it [Response], half hoping that something good will come on. If it does, you are happy for another half hour. If not, then you start an evening-long spiral of frustration and even greater exhaustion. In the end, instead of rejuvenating yourself you become frustrated and irritable [Effect].

You know better, yet you keep repeating this cycle, increasing your frustration and irritation, and even start to feel depressed as the hours slip by because you realize you have just wasted the only personal time you have. When you finally rise from the couch you're more tired than when you started your evening of television, only now you feel bad that you just wasted an entire evening doing nothing. The Cause of this is not that there was nothing good on the television. The Cause was your decision to not turn the television off. The Cause of your ruined evening was your not breaking your old cycle.

Imagine what your evening could have been had you been living mindfully. If you had the wherewithal to step back from the events of your life, you would have been able to see the cycle that was going on around you, and you could have made the decision to do something else. The difference is being aware of your choices in life. The decision is still yours to make. You are still in control of your life. In fact you are in greater control of your life, because you can now make a decision that is in YOUR best interest.

The crucial element in turning a bad decision into a good one lies in your ability to pause your auto-pilot between the **Ca**use of whatever event is going on and your **R**esponse to it. You do this by living mindfully. Living mindfully will give you the separation you need in your life so that you can hit the pause button and make choices that are in your best interest, rather than just for your immediate gratification.

In looking back at our television example, you could have chosen to take a nap. You could have chosen to read a book. You could have gone to the gym. You could have listened to music. But instead you made a choice to watch television because that is "just what you do." And that is the problem you can change through Proper Breathing, Daily Meditation and Mindful Living.

Every day you are given real opportunities to change your life. They do not come in the form of clouds parting and seas opening up. They do not come in the form of high drama screaming matches television and movie producers are so fond of. Instead they are given to you in the little choices that you must make every day. Those are the choices that direct your life and either land you at the right place at the right time, or leave you at the end of a dead end alley wondering how you ever got there. Every time you have a choice to make, you can act quickly and rashly, or you can take a minute to consider the consequences and make the right choice.

I often hear people say, "But I have to act fast and make split decisions. My life depends on it." Really? When was the last time you had to make a split second decision in order to live? Even our most highly trained special forces don't act on rash decisions. They are trained to do exactly the opposite; to pause, to think and to do the right thing. It's the difference between taking careful aim and doing what they call "spray and pray." Firing in a panic without aiming, hoping to hit the target, which rarely happens.

Oh, and don't worry, if a truck is barreling down at you out of control I am very confident that your cortex will jump into action and get you out of the way. If a car swerves into your lane I am sure you will yank your wheel to avoid it. Your brain stem is good in those situations. But if you make good choices before you even get there, if you leave more space between you and the next car, if you give yourself a buffer in life, you can avoid putting yourself in those situations in the first place. You could have looked both ways before crossing the street and seen the truck from a safe distance. All of which would have prevented you from being forced to make a life-saving decision.

If you ever find yourself walking out of a bar having had too much to drink, you are forced to make a decision. You either have to drive home drunk, and risk hurting someone or getting pulled over, or you have to pay for an expensive taxi. Being forced into this situation was not the result of just having too much to drink. It was the result of a series of choices that you made along the way.

First, you decided to go into a bar knowing you had to drive home. Second you had the first drink, knowing it would lower your will power and increase your chances of having a second. Third, you had the third drink knowing it would set you over the legal limit. You see my point. The decision whether or not to drink and drive was not a stand-alone decision. It was the result of a series of bad choices that happened long before.

Should you watch television or read a book? Should you work yourself to exhaustion or take time to recharge and refresh? Should you eat a salad or dig into a cheeseburger? These are simple choices that have profound effects on your life. Just think how different your life would be if you stopped for a moment before making a choice to ensure it was the right one.

We all know what the right choices are. If you are unsure, then the next chapter will help you to find what the right ones are for you. It will help you find your own Simple Truth so that you can start to live by them. The next time you have a choice to make, commit to taking a moment to use **CaRE** so that you can make good choices. Those are the choices that will change your life and help you evolve.

Exercise – Playtime Meditation

Most people have a problem when they start to meditate. They take it too seriously. Rather than relaxing, they become stressed by the idea of wanting it to be a perfect experience. They get nervous about not doing it correctly, worried that they are going to make a mistake. In trying to create a perfect meditation practice, they end up missing the imperfection that is unavoidably the human mind.

If this sounds like you, then take a breath and stop yourself from paying attention to all the distracting details some people attach to meditation. Don't worry about candles or alters. Don't worry about soundtracks or curtains. Simply sit down, put a small smile on your face and breathe. That is really the best way to start.

Seeing, greeting and accepting yourself are all a part of meditation, and there is no way to prepare you for that other than by simply sitting and breathing.

The beauty of meditation is that there is no wrong way to do it. Sure, you may not be doing it as deeply or as easily as a devotee who has been turning inward for twenty years. But, guess what. You are not that devotee. You are you. You will have a slightly different experience meditating than anyone else will have.

The good thing is that nobody else will know what is going on in your head while you meditate, so nobody will really know if you're doing it wrong.

So, before you start a "serious" meditation practice, set aside some playtime to meditate. After all, playtime was the way we all learned about the basics of life. So why not use it to learn again?

Select a time in the morning when you first wake up and start by spending just 3 minutes in a playful and light meditation each day. You can go in the bathroom and close the door to do this. You can sit up or in your bed and start with some simple breaths. Don't expect anything from it, but accept what comes.

Start by smiling as you close your eyes. Do not think about meditation. Instead just think about keeping a smile on your face as you take the first several breaths.

Breathe in and out deeply as I have described and focus on the corner of your lips and how they come together when you smile.

Don't worry about the clock. You may become frustrated by your inability to stop your mind from throwing words and thoughts into your meditation. Don't try to stop it. Think of it as a game, a game between you and your own mind, your own inner voice. When a thought comes into your head, focus on the corners of your smile to yourself and say "thought." Then let it slide by and evaporate like smoke.

How can one minute help you? Scientists actually see changes to the brain with a minimum of time spent meditating. While you want to build up to a longer practice of ten minutes or more with every sitting, learn to enjoy the benefits that come from just a short meditation at different times in your day. Learn to use these mini-meditations as a way to release your stress and maintain a balance.

This is by no means an end-all, but a start-to a growing practice. Just as a single baby step does not constitute walking, starting there can lead to running marathons. The key is to keep at it, and the best way to do that is to have fun with it in smaller doses.

Exercise – Mindful Eating

Mindful Eating is a simple exercise you can do at any meal. I first practiced it by myself when my sense of smell and taste first came back during my recovery. It was as if every molecule was a vibrant source of pleasure. I still practice it when I am forced to eat alone while traveling. I use this as a way to center myself, and to regain my appreciation for the food I am enjoying.

This is such a powerful exercise, that it is now being used by dieticians as a way to increase awareness among their patients of what, and how much, a person is eating.

For this exercise, pick a time when you are eating alone. It could be breakfast when nobody is around. It could be at a lunchroom table. It could be dinner in a hotel restaurant while traveling. Where you are is not important. Being alone and able to focus is.

If you are eating a salad for lunch, take a deep breath and center yourself in your seat. Continue to breathe in and out as you focus your actions on your breath just like your meditation practice.

Become aware of the world around you. Feel yourself in your seat, feel the pressure of your body pressing down into the chair. Before you pick up your fork, take a breath and consider the salad in front of you. Consider the lettuce, the tomatoes and the vegetables. Look at the meat, the cheese, and whatever else there is before you. Smell the dressing and the herbs in your salad. Say to yourself "arugula," "tuna fish", "parmesan" as you see each ingredient. Just recognize that each is there.

When you reach for your fork, be aware of your arm extending and reaching. Be aware of your fingers as they touch the handle. Be aware of the sensation that your fingers have when they touch the metal.

Before you raise the greens to your mouth, look at them, notice their color, shape, smell and texture. Appreciate them for what they are.

When you bite into them, feel your teeth penetrate and focus your attention on their texture and their taste. Taste the tuna fish, the cheese and the lettuce. Separate each flavor in your mouth as you start to chew. When you chew, be aware of the sensation of your teeth against your food, of your tongue inside your cheeks and the flavors and textures of the food you have just eaten.

Chew your food slowly as you breathe and be aware of all the sensations around and inside of you. When you swallow, feel the food move down your esophagus and into your stomach. Notice the changes that happen to your body as you continue with your meal, breaking down each action as it occurs and paying attention to the details and sensations you experience.

If you get distracted, just return to your meal and your mindful eating. Take the time to learn to be aware of your actions, as well as the sensations that you derive from the world around you. Learn to not take even the simplest tasks for granted. Also, be aware of how much control you have over your actions when you slow down and take the time to really notice them.

Step 3: Find YOUR Simple Truth

Find YOU inside of you

There are two entities within each of us. There is the "you" that people see and interact with every day. The person they recognize from your driver's license and Facebook photos. The easily recognizable person that everyone knows you to be on the outside, who wakes up, goes to work, logs onto your computer and lives your life. You are the personality that everyone has learned to be comfortable with.

Then there is the real YOU that lives deep with your core. This is the real "YOU." It is the entity you were born as, before outside influences affected your opinions and needs. It is the entity that you were born to be, free from the layers that have created the you everyone knows. You keeps the real YOU hidden, even from your closest circle of friends, because you have trained yourself to do so. From time to time YOUR true personality comes out in a moment of happiness and bliss. Not necessarily when you let your hair down, but when you are simply being real without any pretenses.

Every culture and religion refers to the real YOU in some way, shape or form. It is sometimes called the dharma, soul, ki, consciousness, or the spirit. Some even call it God – the one you touch when you reach deep within yourself. I prefer to call this entity the real YOU so that there are no religious connotations attached to the idea of being YOURSELF.

I'm sure this is not the first time you have heard the phrase: just be YOURSELF. It is no wonder that we hear it so often. We have all been trained to keep to society's rules rather than to be YOURSELF. We have, in effect, learned to keep OURSELVES hidden very well, for fear of reprisal.

As you start to boot up your Simple Truth, you will be introduced to your true self one step at a time. As you slowly remove the layers of doubt, indecision and outside influences that have covered the real YOU over the years, you will get closer to your true self, your own Simple Truth and the life YOU have been looking for. The closer you get, the more you see, and the greater will be your evolution toward YOUR true self.

Simple Truth

You do not have a soul. You are a soul who happens to reside inside the body you are familiar with.

As you start to see the real YOU, you will find it easier to use that knowledge to continue removing everything that is not YOU; the influences, the fears and the anger that has been preventing you from living YOUR life. With those influences gone, you can start to act in a way that is true to who YOU are. That will enable you to get around your old programming and truly evolve.

Meditation is one of the tools that will help you do this. It will ground you and give you the awareness you need to find out just who YOU are, so that you can get past the layers that have been preventing you from being true to YOURSELF. Your journey will be an eye opening experience. It will undoubtedly be an emotional experience. It certainly was for me. But freeing yourself like this will enable you to be in charge of your actions and live the life YOU want.

It may be confusing at first. But the distinction between you and YOU is a critical one. It is one that you must make if you want to evolve and live YOUR own life. If you're not sure about the separation between you and YOU, take a moment to think about your life. How many times in the past year have you said "this isn't me," or "this isn't what I want to do?" How many times have you said to yourself "I'm not comfortable with this," thinking that you would be more comfortable taking a different approach to a problem? If you have ever doubted your actions because they went against your integrity or your beliefs, that is an example of your two selves coming into conflict. It is an example of your inner self trying to reach out and say "this isn't being true to YOURSELF."

The YOU that I am speaking of is not the same thing as that inner voice that you are learning to override. It is your true self that you have learned to over shadow with 40,000 years of programming. It is your innate nature that should have been the guiding force in your life but you have learned to block by the ever growing list of habits, social mores, distractions and influences that have gotten you to where you are right now. Through meditation you will find the strength and stability you need to reconnect with YOUR true self and help return YOUR life to you.

After you have begun meditating on a regular basis, you will notice that you enter a state free of distraction and outside influence. You will feel empty and at the same time filled with YOUR true nature. Some call this being in touch with God. Others call it reaching into your own consciousness. In both cases this is the moment when you are closest to YOUR real self. While your body pauses in your meditation YOUR true self will expand. Your consciousness will grow and your true spirit will start to emerge. YOU will become more aware of who you are and where you are.

All of this will open your consciousness and enable you to override your old programming so that you can start to live life based on your own Simple Truth. In doing so, you will evolve into the person you were meant to be.

YOU Are Your World

There is a world that only you can control. It is a universe called YOU. As much as you would like to think otherwise, everything that exists outside of the Universe of YOU is beyond your control. You have no power over what goes on in the world around you. You can only manage how you respond to it. When you get into a car, you can look both ways before pulling out of your garage, you can put on a seatbelt and make sure your airbag light is active, but in the end, there is little you can do if a drunk driver recklessly speeds around the corner and runs into you.

As much as you may try to influence the world around you, you cannot control what happens out there. You can only respond to the events as they occur. You can either panic or you can stay calm. You can either react by habit, or you can start to manage your life and your experience. Only YOU have a say over what you do.

If you are trying to live a life of happiness you will only find your happiness within YOURSELF. If you wait for the world to fall in line with your idea of happiness, you will undoubtedly be waiting for a long, long time. That is because they world around you is led by an endless number of influences, of which you play a very small part.

In the end, the outside world will remain outside of your influence. It will disappoint, it will challenge, and it will seek its own balance which will rarely have your best interest in mind.

What you have to realize is that you do not have to live your life to fit the world around you. You do not have to respond in the same way that you always have. You can smile, take a breath and decide to follow YOUR own path at any time. Remember that YOU have the power over what you do. YOU can direct your ego. You can choose to not engage in any activity that you don't want to. And because of that you can always walk away. The choice is yours because you only have to answer to one person – YOURSELF.

I am constantly asked at what point do you keep walking away or backing down from a confrontation. The answer is as long as you want to. In the end, you do not have to put yourself in a situation where you are going to be trapped into taking a specific action or feeling like you are backing down if you don't. By being aware of who you are and where you are, and by not letting your ego get in the way, you can always make the right choice for yourself. You can always avoid a confrontation.

If you are sitting somewhere enjoying a beautiful sunset and someone else is being too loud, you have a choice. You can let your ego take over and see their actions as a personal affront to you. You can confront them and ruin your evening, or you can take a breath and remember that you cannot control everything around you. You can fume about how this person is disrupting "your" sunset, or you can change your mindset and think about how wonderful it is that everyone is out enjoying the world together and in their own way. You can embrace the fact that people are different or enjoy the fact that there is give and take in every situation. Remember, you cannot control the world around you. You can only control how you respond.

Let me ask you a question. If it was raining outside, would you be happy? If it was cold outside, could you still enjoy the day? Would you still be a happy person? Or would you be miserable because of the weather? Can you only be happy if it is sunny and eighty degrees? If so, then be prepared to have your life ruled by something entirely out of your control.

The alternative to letting your life be ruled by the world around you is to accept that the weather is a factor, like so many others in your life. It is a part of the balance that holds the world together, but it is not something that will make or break your ability to enjoy life. If everything that you are depends on the environment around you being perfect, then you will forever be unhappy. Understand that the world is an imperfect place. That it is human nature to want it to be perfect. But also understand that your desire for perfection is the result of your programming, not your real need. Your true self is happy regardless of the weather, or the people around you, or the world you find yourself, if you allow it to be.

So instead of fighting the world around you, learn to respond, not by habit and old programming, but by grounding yourself in YOUR true self. Be aware of who you are and where you are, so that you can smile in your own skin no matter what you find before you.

Always Be Aware of Who YOU Are

Look around. No matter where you are, you really do live in a pretty wonderful world. It is not perfect. But then nothing ever is. Until, that is, you allow yourself to see the imperfections of the world as part of its perfection. Each of those imperfections gives the world flexibility. Each allows the world to bend to the needs of different people. So while it is not absolutely perfect for anyone, it is pretty darn nice for everyone.

The problem is not the imperfections of the world, but in your ability to accept them. You see, YOU are watching the world through layers of frustration, anger, despair and hope. All of which come from past memories and future expectations. All of those shade your perception of reality. They cause you to focus on the seeming imperfections of the world, which is a large part of your unhappiness. Your unhappiness is not due to living in dismal circumstances, but to your perception of your circumstances.

Your ability to look past your own fears and desires, your hopes and expectations is the difference between seeing the wonderful world of opportunities that really do exist, or seeing a dreary trap. It is the difference between seeing what is important in the world, and being distracted by imperfections that really don't matter in the long run.

Have you ever had a day when you just woke up sad and distraught, where the world seemed dull and monochromatic? Perhaps you had just broken up with someone you cared about and viewed life as an emotional dead end. Have you ever experienced the feeling of elation after the person you just broke up with reached out to you? At the moment you heard that persons' voice, the world probably shifted for you. It suddenly became a bright place of hope and renewal.

The world didn't change. You did. Your perceptions changed. The world was a happier place at that moment because you decided it was going to be. And yes, living in a happy world really is that simple. You can decide at any point in time to be happy or to be distraught. You can choose to see the world as a place for endless opportunities, or for ceaseless dead ends.

This is why being aware of who you are, is so important to being happy. If you know who you are and know how to ground yourself in that knowledge, then you can define the way in which you experience your life.

Simple Truth

The greatest struggle you will ever face is simply being YOU.

The world around you can be a wonderful place if you let it. Because your life is not fixed in somebody else's idea of perfection, you have the ability to define what is important and what is not. You can do this based on your own dharma, your own perception of the world. The fact that the world, and the universe for that matter, exists in an ever changing balance of imperfection means that you can determine how you want to live in it; if, that is, you know who you are and what you want.

If you were to take a huge step back and look at the earth from a great distance, you would see that we actually live on a tiny speck of dust, hurling through the universe at about 540,000 miles an hour. The only protection against the sun's radiation and killer asteroids is an impossibly thin and fragile layer of gas we majestically call our atmosphere.

Life on this planet has survived cataclysmic asteroids and meteors in the past. We have lived through ice ages and periods of global warming that make our worst wars seem trivial by comparison. We will continue to live through more of the same. If you can look past your immediate issues you will not be able to stop yourself from marveling at the miracle that life even exists on this planet at all.

I remind myself of this every time someone cuts me off while driving or tries to bruise my ego with an aside. It centers me and helps me realize how insignificant these things are in the grander scheme of things. It also reminds me to look inward for my happiness. Because that is the only thing any of us have control over.

You cannot control the potential cataclysms of the universe. You cannot control what another driver does on the road. You can only control the choices you make and the way in which you respond to the world around you. You can guide both toward those elements in your life that will make you happy. But doing so starts with knowing yourself from the inside out.

This chapter is designed to help introduce you to YOU. It will also help you recognize those feelings, emotions and habits that are not YOU. It is not a one-time exercise. It is an ongoing, never ending process of being aware of who you are, where you are and what will bring you happiness.

How you define yourself will change as you evolve. Your sense of self will mature as you mature. So do not worry if your view of yourself today is different from how you viewed yourself ten years ago. It should be different. It will be different ten years from now. That difference only means that you are truly living.

So be aware of who you are no matter where you are. Be aware of what you want and what you do not want. Most important, be aware that the only thing that is constant in life is change. So throughout the changes that life will put you through, knowing who YOU are is the only way for YOU to guide yourself in the direction that you want to go and to empower you to make good choices along the way.

Your Time

Let's start by taking five minutes for a simple exercise. Open up a tape measure and extend it to eighty inches. That is the average lifespan of a person, give or take a few years. Now, measure out your age in inches. Do you see what is left? That is how much time you most likely have. Sure, you may live past that. You may also get hit by a bus before it. Just realize that if you are forty-five years old you most likely have thirty-five years left, on average, to live your life. Also realize that everything, every precious memory, every little adventure, everything that you know or have done to this point has been rolled into whatever inches you measured out. If you are only half-way there, then you could do everything that you have ever experienced all over again. If you are in your twenties, you can live all of your current experiences four more times.

This exercise is not about the specter of death. It is about understanding that life is about more than having a pulse. It is about living your time to the fullest. This should be your wakeup call. No matter how many inches you have left, your life is far from over. Even if you only have a few years remaining, or even a few days, why would you want to spend them doing anything less than by being true to YOURSELF?

Every six months, for the rest of my life, I'm going to have to get an MRI to see if any new tumors are growing in my head or on my spine. It's a twice-yearly reminder of how fragile the freedom of living is for me. So ask yourself, if you could have lived your life differently, how would you have changed the way you lived? More important, from this day forward how will you live your life?

You are not locked into making the same choices you have in the past. You have the experience to know what you like and don't like. So how will you live your remaining inches to ensure they give you the experience and the life that you actually want?

Remember, the only thing that is constant in life is change. So always remember the tape measure, always remember where you are in life and think about whether what you are doing is the best thing to do. If you can remind yourself from time to time about those things that are truly important to you, you will never have to worry about wandering too far from yourself or getting caught following your old programming.

Your Space

Many years ago, when I was practicing martial arts, somebody asked me how many fights I had been in. I responded that aside from competitions, none. I was fortunate to have trained under two very traditional teachers – Grand Master Bong Soo Han and World Seido founder Tadashi Nakamura. Both believed that meditation was a crucial part of any martial art, and that self control was an essential part of any martial arts training.

During one session with Grand Master Bong Soo Han, I remember a student asked him "what is the best move if someone attacks you?" Master Bong Soo Han smiled and answered "you run way." The student pressed, "what if you were trapped in a corner?" "What if you were surrounded by a gang?" He replied "learn to never put yourself in a place where you are forced to fight in the first place then it will never be a problem. But if after everything you do, you still find yourself in a bad situation, just run away."

When the student kept pressing him, he smiled and said, "This training is not meant for fighting. It should give you the confidence so that you never have to prove anything to anyone. You should always be in control and know that you always have the choice to walk away. If you are aware of the world around you, you will never find yourself in a position where you have to fight."

I have found no better explanation for the world we all live in – physically or mentally. As long as you get rid of that instinctive impulse to hit back, you never have to find yourself in a position where you are forced to do so. This is not the same as living a passive life. It means living a very active life. Just one that doesn't require violence to get what you want. It requires being actively aware, mindful and present at all times. But it also means taking a very compassionate approach to your life. One in which you shape your destiny, rather than have someone else shape it for you.

> ***Simple Truth***
>
> *What people say is their karma. What you say back is yours.*

Today dangers come in many different forms – they are more intellectual than physical. They have longer term ramifications than just short-term results. This does not mean they are any less damaging. They simply have taken another form.

Because of this, your personal space needs to change with the modern times. Instead of monitoring how far people are from you physically, you also need to monitor how close they are getting to you mentally. Rarely does someone just start attacking you out of the blue. It escalates from insults to bruised ego to action. So ask yourself, at what point does an insult require a response? The answer by the way is never.

As Grand Master Bon Soo Han used to teach us, the human arm and leg are only so long. As long as you stay far enough away from someone else, as long as you keep out of their reach, that person will never be a threat to you. So you never have to engage them. All you have to do is step backward every time they step forward.

The same holds true in all aspects of your life. Rather than striking out at anything that threatens you, you need to pause and think if that something is an actual threat, or just a bruise to your ego. You need to create a mental space to buffer yourself from the outside world. It will enable you to establish a comfort zone so you can prevent yourself from running after battles that just don't need to be fought or opportunities that are not in your best interest.

If you are aware of your own mental and physical comfort zones, and can apply that to your surroundings, you will always be YOU, a being in the world able to interact with it on your terms. Your actions will always be your choice.

Your Emotions

Your emotions are the way in which your old programming communicates with you. It's how your operating system translates the subtle, and not so subtle, threats of the world into action that you can understand. If you feel anger, it's your fight or flight response without the need for immediate action. If you feel hatred, it's your body's way of sending a warning to the need for possible future action. If you feel kinship, it's your body's way of saying, this person is okay.

As much as you may try to hide them or ignore them, your emotions are as much a part of you as your skin and your hair. You may think you can hide them behind a poker face, but they are far more visible than you may think. They have a way of coming out in your eyes, your posture and the little movements you are not even aware of. No matter how well you think you can cover them up, they are a part of who you are. So you need to be aware of your emotions in order to understand what your programming is trying to tell you, if you are to act with your best interests in mind.

When someone pushes one of your buttons that makes you angry or upset, you need to realize what is happening inside of you. It's the first step to pausing and thinking before you react.

When I feel an emotion rising I take a moment and work through a mini-script I created. I ask myself, "What am I feeling?" It's a way for me to remind myself that my emotions are not who I am; they are an early warning system that connects me with the world around me. I then ask "why?" I want to make sure that I am making a conscious decision whether to act on my emotions or not. Just because I am feeling something does not mean I have to take action on it. Nor do I have to feed into someone else's emotions. I have the choice how much energy I direct to an emotion or not. After all, whatever emotion I feel is mine, and I can do with it what I want.

Simple Truth

Don't let yourself jump to a response. Take a breath. Ground yourself. There is always time to do the right thing.

I also remind myself of the 180 degree rule. This simply means that in most cases, whatever someone says about you is really a reflection of their own feelings. If they are trying to disrespect you, it is because they are reflecting their own feelings of being disrespected. If someone is trying to make you feel bad, it is because they are trying to get rid of their own feelings of worthlessness. This is part of our programming. It is how we deal with feeling inferior. We mirror those feelings on to others.

My inner conversation used to go something like this:

> Unbelievable! This person is so far out of line. They're completely off base. I cannot believe they just said that. I want to strike out and yell back. I want to put them in their place.
>
> Wait, okay, before I start yelling, what made me so angry? Well, this person put me down. They're not showing me the respect I have earned.

Am I sure I deserve respect? Of course I do. Then I already have it. I'm the only one that can respect or disrespect me. As long as I'm okay with who I am, then what they say is inconsequential. It's almost absurd. They're just trying to feel good about themselves, which makes me laugh.

And laugh I usually do. I laugh because it's my way to diffuse any situation; and right there is when I can take the emotions out of my response. Because if I know my own Simple Truth, I can remain above whatever it is someone says.

How do you do that? By refusing to engage someone at their level you will realize that there is rarely a reason to be angry or need to prove them wrong. Much as Grand Master Bong Soo Han taught us in the physical world, as long as you take ego and emotion out of the mental world, rarely is there ever a need to engage someone. As long as you keep the emotional aspect out of a discussion, any confrontation can be diffused. You can always walk away.

What is important though is that you use each emotional blowup as a tool. As a way to look back to ask yourself why you got so emotional about whatever comment was said. Ask yourself "what were you feeling?" If you were angry, was it really because of the comment? Or did it strike a chord with you? Did it remind you of some event in your past? You need to ask yourself, when was the last time you reacted like this? When was the last time you felt this way?

Tuck it away for when you have a moment and try to remember what the conversations or circumstances were like in those instances. If you can find the triggers that set off an emotion within you, then you have a very powerful tool. You can start to find the emotional pattern in your life. And that pattern can then be dealt with.

Perhaps it goes back to childhood when your schoolmates teased you, or perhaps when a family member put you down with casual asides. If you can trace your emotions back to the triggers that set you off, you can prevent them from ruling your life.

Take a moment to write down the different emotions that tend to set you off. Write down the instances in which those emotions rise out of control. Find the pattern that causes you to act like someone you don't want to act like and start being the person you were meant to be, before the layers turned YOU into you.

Your Social Sphere

Humans are social creatures. We gravitate toward other people because it is our nature. We seek out the approval of those around us because human contact is important to our very survival. It always has been and always will be. It is a strength that helped us band together and survive for thousands of years. But at times our need for approval can trap us into a social circle that is more constricting than supporting.

No matter how old you are you have accumulated some very unique and valuable life experiences. You have tried things that nobody else has tried. You have won. You have lost. You have lived. Yet at different times in your life, deep down inside you may still feel like you are still a kid in high-school with just as many insecurities and fears as you had back then. As if all of your life experiences were for naught. Do you ever catch yourself sitting in a meeting or perhaps at a party, thinking to yourself:

> "I am so out of my league right now. Just look at all the people around me. They have ten or fifteen years on me. They have all done big deals and played with the heavy hitters. What have I done? I'm just a kid compared to them."

We all do it. It is natural part of your wiring, your programming. In a way it's your body telling you that you're out of your element and your comfort zone. That was an emotional warning that worked well hundreds of years ago, but in today's world, may not be quite as relevant.

When you hear that voice rise up, you need to ground yourself and realize where you are and what you are saying. Not only is this your nagging inner voice rising up, it is something worse. It is you allowing your operating system to forget everything that you have accomplished, sending you back to being that scared teenager you first saw during your first few days of school.

Everyone felt like that, and still feels like that now from time to time. Everyone still has those feelings of doubt and that primordial need to be the one on top. But no matter how young or old you are, you are not the kid you once were. In fact, you never were that naive! You were just scared then, as you are now. Today you have experience, you have knowledge, and you bring something important to the table. If you did not, you would not be where you are.

If you are to grow, you have to understand you will always feel inadequate from time to time. There will be days where you question yourself, as you should. This is a natural response to the world around you. But you also need to know that everyone around that table or at that party feels exactly the same way. They are comparing themselves to you, trying to find your strengths and your weaknesses. They are scrambling to find their own place in the imaginary social strata. They will try to keep you out of their circle, no matter what the situation is, until they no longer consider you a threat. It is the way we worked thousands of years ago, and it is the way most people operate now.

So stop. Today, you have a choice. You don't have to live in a tribe if you don't want to. Your survival is not wholly dependent on fitting in. Today, your happiness is based on your ability to recognize what makes you happy. Not on your ability to attach yourself to someone, or something else. If you base your happiness on a social badge or varsity jacket, then if that badge is ever taken away you will instantly be returned to your miserable self. You will never be in control of your own life. So why would you ever put yourself in that position?

It's wonderful to have friends. Friends support and nurture you. Friends help you grow. They don't stifle you in order to keep their own social structure alive. Being able to step out of a social situation with an understanding and awareness of who you are, what you value, and what you want is the difference between being happy no matter where you end up and having your happiness reliant on the whims of others. So "know thyself," "to thine own self be true," because that is what will make your life your own. That is what will enable you to live by your own Simple Truth. Not at the whim of someone else's values, or lack of them.

Take a moment to write down some things that you like and don't like. Write down the music you enjoy, art you like, authors you have loved. Do not do it based on what is popular, but what you truly enjoy when you are by yourself. Get to know yourself. Say hello to YOU.

Write down traits that are important to YOU, that make you feel good about yourself. Start a list that will help you establish the standards by which you will value your friends and your life. They will help you define yourself and the social settings that will support you. Who knows, they may even help you create your own tribe.

Be Comfortable in YOUR World

Have you ever seen someone behind the wheel that tries to outrace everyone at the light? Have you ever seen the look in that driver's face? It is usually a mix of rage, fear, panic and desperation. Either that or it is an attempt to look cool while trying to mask those same emotions. Do you know where that driver is in ten minutes? That's right, maybe fifty yards further than you are. And during those fifty yards that driver has been in a constant panic. They have been searching for a gap ahead of them. They have been looking over their shoulder to make sure the police aren't watching them. They scream if another car edges up on them and gloat if they make a few extra feet. They are no different than our ancestors from 40,000 years ago.

Along the way, they anger other drivers, irritate other people, and have lost control of their own lives. They have risked fender benders and wrecks, all for fifty yards. Soon enough the inevitable happens. Other drivers start to close ranks and inevitably stop letting them edge into their lanes. Horns will start to honk and everyone's stress levels start to rise. You see how something as small as driving down a street can quickly mirror the larger rat race we all get trapped in? What starts out as an attempt to get ahead at the cost of everyone else, not only endangers their own success, it starts to work against them.

Life is like that. When you start to claw your way ahead of others, sooner or later the world starts to claw back. Rarely is the goal you set out to accomplish achieved. Even if you do achieve it, you cannot rest. You will always have to look over your shoulder for the person who wants your position. The worst part is you are no longer living your life. You are back where your ancestors were, responding to the challenges, real and imagined that occur around you.

> ***Simple Truth***
>
> *Seek inspiration on the outside, but everything you need is within you.*

It starts by smothering your own personal style in order to fit in. Or perhaps you act differently so that you don't stand out. Soon enough you will have a moment where you feel like you are acting rather than actually living. That is because it is exactly what you are doing.

Rarely does living someone else's life happen overnight. The changes are slow but progressive. Yes, in the end, you lose yourself to the collective around you, and rarely are the benefits worth the costs you incur to get to where you once thought you wanted to go. Those that actually achieve whatever goal they started out in search of, quickly find out that it was not what they were ultimately after. It is why so many striving actors, brokers, artists and musicians end with their lives in such a mess. It is also why we marvel at those that have figured it out, and live their lives on their own terms, usually out of the spotlight.

So let me ask you. What is it you want to achieve? What kind of lifestyle would make you happy? More important, is it your life that you are looking to live? Or the life someone else convinced you that you want?

Throughout much of my life I had what I thought were goals only to find that once I had achieved them they were far from what I thought they would be. I charged into college with the dream of a degree that would guarantee my success. I achieved that degree. But my degree assured me of nothing more than a job and a career that could not have been more wrong for me.

I left New York City for Los Angeles and a career in film. I achieved that. But it was not really where I wanted to be doing. I helped start the first website for the Los Angeles Times, I ran a leading agency, and I built a successful company from the ground up. I had the healthy six figure salary and the trappings I was looking for. But none of this was really what I wanted. Because as soon as I got what I thought I wanted, I then started working for a seven figure salary and a larger apartment. You see, it never stops.

In the end what I wanted was very simple. So simple, it is almost comical. I simply wanted to be happy. What I did not realize was that you can never truly be happy if your happiness depends on someone else's ideas or on an outside factor. Beating every car to the next light may have made me smile for a bit, but sooner or later someone else cut in front of me, and then I was right back where I started – looking for the next opportunity.

Having an expensive car may make you feel superior for a while. But it will not make you happy. Soon enough you will want a newer, shinier, faster one. Having a mansion will not make you happy. Soon enough you will want a larger one with a better pool and a better zip code.

Before you know it, you are playing the same game you have probably played most of your life. You have been responding to your old programming in an effort to keep up with the Joneses.

You have fallen into the same trap most people fall into – mistaking short-term elation for long-term happiness.

The next time you want to do something that you think will make you happy, play a little game and ask yourself why? From my experience it will probably go something like this:

> I need a new apartment. Why? Because I have lived in this one for five years and I am tired of it. Why? Because my old one no longer reflects who I am now. I have grown and matured and I need something that is more "me." Why? Because when I walk in from a long day at work I want something that will make me happy. Why? Because I want to feel good about all the hard work I put into my job. Why? Because my job does not really make me feel happy, it makes me satisfied, but also nervous and on edge if I lose it and all of this.

Or perhaps it may go something like this:

> I really like this person I just met. Why? Because they make me laugh, they make me smile. Why? Because they make me feel special. Why? Because they make me forget about all the problems I have, they make me look at all the wonderful things I have achieved rather than my faults and flaws.

For most of us, our happiness is predicated on some outside influence. By itself, that is not entirely bad. But it is fleeting. When that person or that job goes away so does your happiness. Just because you can project an image of success or happiness to everyone around us, does not mean you are happy.

Being happy is far simpler than that. It is not a goal that you have to chase after. It is a feeling, a state of mind that comes from doing the right things in your life. It is the result of your actions, not a goal in and of itself.

If status and ego were not a factor in your happiness, then you could probably take a lower paying job that gave you better peace of mind. This is where the trade-offs always comes into play. What is the value between your success or even your long-term security and your immediate happiness? That is where the real choices need to be made.

Let's be honest. You live in a society with a range of comforts. But you have to work, pay bills, and pay taxes to live in it. There are also variable responsibilities, such as building up a retirement fund, which you need to keep in mind. The reality is there is a cost to having running water. There is a cost to having heat and electricity. There is a cost to living with the basic luxuries of the modern world. If you do not want these luxuries, then you are always free to leave and wander the world.

However if you read the news at all, the realities of living in these places usually make them less than appealing. Living there means living like humans did hundreds of years ago. Some places are more similar to the dark ages than the modern world. Bad water causes dysentery, warlords kill indiscriminately, and the poor are raped and pillaged without fear of retribution. There is no food like we know food, there is no restful sleep, and there is no wine or beer, no fresh fruit.

If you think this is not an accurate picture, then just consider how people survive in the third world. Haiti, Uganda and even Afghanistan portray some of the realities that I do not think most of you want to experience. I'm not saying we shouldn't all do our best to help those in need. But I am saying that most of us could not even imagine living in the day-to-day realities of those conditions. Even if you could survive comfortably there, the daily struggles would leave little time to find the inner peace and happiness you are currently seeking.

The answer to finding your own happiness does not lie in either of the two extremes; the first in spending your way to happiness, the second in hiding from the responsibilities of today's society. The answer lies in finding your own place of harmony between the two. What Buddha called the middle road. To do this means knowing who YOU really are and then recalibrating your expectations so that you can put your time and energy into the aspects of your life that are most important to YOU – financially, spiritually and ecumenically. Only then can you find the right kind of balance that will lead to your happiness.

Happiness is not about feeling elated and euphoric every single minute of the day. Happiness is not about never-ending joy. Happiness is about creating harmony throughout your life so that you are content and, well, happy.

You need to find a job that makes you feel good about the work you do and that makes you feel good about yourself. It may not pay millions, but that is not the point. The point is that you enjoy it, that you gain from it, and that it compensates you for your time – financially and spiritually. You do not need a mansion to be happy. Nor do you need to live in a perpetual state of nirvana.

You need a home that you can enjoy and that does not create more stress in mortgages and payments than you can afford. You do not need a boyfriend or girlfriend that makes you look great in family photographs if they make you feel inadequate or demand you be someone you are not. You need someone who will help you live your dreams and help you maintain your own happiness, just as you will support their dreams and their efforts to find their happiness.

Each of you has been given a gift to live in the world we are all a part of. Each of you is blessed to have landed on this speck of dirt we call Earth. So use those gifts to your benefit and to the benefit of those around you. Use your time to help others. Use your time to help yourself. But use your time in a way that creates your own happiness, rather than trying to control those things that you really have no control over in the first place.

Travel Your Path But Live In Your World

After all the doubt, the anger, the pain, and the realization I felt from having to stop my life for almost a year, of having my life waylaid by something I could not control, I started to think about the specter of death. It was nothing morbid or unnatural. To me it was just being realistic.

I did not tell very many people about the sixth tumor that was still inside my head. It was close to my optic lobes and, as my surgeon explained, it would be a more difficult surgery with potentially life altering side effects. My doctors, and rightly so, had decided not to operate on it immediately. Instead we would monitor it with quarterly MRIs. I asked them what would happen if we did nothing. To which he replied "if it continues to grow, it would eventually block the venal draining for your brain."

He was puzzled by my next question, "and then what."

He almost laughed at the absurdity of the question. He was not sure if I was serious. "Well, nobody has ever asked me that. But eventually it would block the body's ability to drain the fluids from your brain and you would eventually die." I smiled to myself at his answer. If I had lived a hundred years ago we would not have even been having this conversation. I would already be dead.

I nodded and bit my thumb. If there was one thing I had learned in business was the importance of considering every option. Even those options that were not desirable were still an option that had to be considered in order to fully understand what was happening.

In a way, I was being handed a tremendous, once in a lifetime choice. I could do absolutely nothing with the remaining tumor knowing that if it grew it could shorten my life or drastically alter it. Or I could make an active change in my life and try to keep it from growing any more. I could choose to do nothing and see what the next cycle of life, or afterlife, had to offer. Or I could change my path and continue on for the next five, ten, forty or more years that might be available to me.

What astounded me the most was that my decision was not an immediate one. I actually spent some time to think it through. Should I take my free ticket? Or should I look for a way to live as long a life as possible? For me it was a profound decision to make. Especially after realizing that I really did not have as much control over my life as I thought I had.

As I thought through my options, I realized no, I did not want to live forever, nor even to an age that many people are now reaching. But I also had more to do. There was more I wanted to do. I had no idea what it was exactly, but I wanted to live MY life for a change, not the one I had been living.

I also realized that the choice I was facing was one every one of us makes every day of our lives. It's just not so real for most of you. It's something that most people aren't forced to face quite so literally.

You see, every day that you wake up you are making this decision. You are choosing to live. Life is not something you are forced to suffer through, it is something you opt into with every breath you breathe and every bite you take. Yet rarely do we recognize making the decision to live. It's as if life is something we take for granted. As if it's something you must suffer through, rather than a conscious choice you make.

This way of thinking is something that you need to change. If you don't want to live, then so be it. But if living is a decision that you have made, then you must take responsibility for how you are going to live your life. Are you going to live it fully? Are you going to live it passionately? Or, are you going to accept a life that you only half live?

This is a choice you must make for the rest of your life. If you decide that you want to live, then you are choosing to do so. And if you are choosing to do so, then you can also choose how to live. Every day that you wake up and smell the air, you are choosing to do so. Every morning that you get out of bed, you are choosing to do so. So realize that every second you are here, you are here by choice. And whether you like it or not, you are in control of your life.

For me, my choice was to change my diet, to cut out processed foods, and start a meditation and yoga practice in earnest. It meant reducing the stress in my life, and in effect starting over. Today, that last tumor is still in my head. It is my own Simple Truth. It has continued to surprise my doctor by simply not growing.

In a way I'm blessed with a very evident signal on how to live my life. You all have similar signals inside of you. Some are physical. Others are emotional. Yours may not grow the same way as mine, but they're there, in the happiness and contentment you enjoy in your life. Learn to listen to yours and to pay attention to them. The choice as to what you do with that information is entirely up to you.

Your Bags Are Already Packed

At some point everyone dreams of running away to a blissful ever after. Why shouldn't you? You start reading about "Happy Ever After" at a very young age. It infuses our movies, our books, our television shows. It even infused our retirement plans. The idea of "Ever After" is why you work so hard. Rarely do you push yourself to enjoy your happy ever right now. Instead you focus on creating an ideal life when you retire. Perhaps you have a plan in the back of your mind to retire to some small farm in the hills to raise goats and make artisanal cheese. Or perhaps you envision opening a restaurant that you can call your own. Maybe you dream of just leaving all of your problems behind and just traveling the world. The question to any of these dreams should not be where you can go, or what can you do, but what will you have when you get there.

Simple Truth

If you take a step back in life, use the experience to take two more forward.

Because no matter what you do or where you go you will still have the same baggage that you have right now. You see, your bags are already packed. The issues and questions you have right now will be with you when you get to wherever you're going. So why not take a look at what you have?

There are those who choose to travel light, not wanting to complicate their lives by dealing with their issues. There are others who thrive on the conflict that they create. Both are wonderful ways to avoid approaching your Simple Truth. Just as with making the choice to live, you also need to choose how you live. You can either live in a stressful environment based on keeping up with the Joneses and running after someone else's dream? Or you can choose to live based on your own needs and your own Simple Truth.

Some of the world's most famous philosophers, poets and prophets left society to find themselves by living alone. One lived in the desert for forty days and nights, another left for the mountains of what is now India. They both came back with a similar thought – you cannot run away from society to find yourself. You have to address your issues in the real world. If you do not, then whenever you return to the cities and towns of your current life, your old issues will still be waiting for you.

This has never been truer than in today's world. Two thousand years ago living in the wild was not all that different than living in a village. There was no running water or central heating. Markets were hardly stocked with the kind of groceries we find on the shelves of modern stores. The luxuries we take for granted simply didn't exist. Unfortunately running away is just not as realistic an answer as it once was.

Since people have been around work and community have always been a part of the human experience, they just changed form. In the beginning survival required that we hunt and forage for food. Later it meant plowing a field, building a shelter, and forming a tribe that could hunt together. Today, you still need to work to survive, and you need a sense of community to survive happily. The difference is with all of the modern conveniences, you now have a much greater choice in what you do and how you do it.

Not all that long ago your choices were pretty much made for you. If you did not hunt or plow you did not eat. If you were in a tribe or clan and did not help out, you were sent off to fend for yourself. In the modern world, if you do not work you cannot pay for food or a place to live, and you are, in effect, banished from the society that you are comfortable in.

So instead of running away, hoping that your baggage will get lost along the way, rethink your strategy. Stay put for a while, and spend some time looking through your baggage. This does not mean you need to force yourself into endless days in a cubicle lit by flickering fluorescents. Instead look at a longer term plan in which you change your life step by step, each one moving you in the direction you want to go.

The beauty is you can choose what kind of society you live in. You can choose your friends and the type of work you do. You don't have to change them all at once. You don't need to throw your life into turmoil. But you are the one who must take control if you want to add happiness and satisfaction onto your salary.

Simple Truth

You may not always pack your bags properly. But it's you who chooses to carry them.

You need to look at the luggage you already have in order to set your expectations so that the journey you are starting on is a realistic one. More important than the destination is the need to live your life in the here and now, and in a realistic way. That will make you happy.

Just remember, there is no simple formula for happiness. Your baggage is different from everyone else's. So don't look for an easy answer. Instead look to rebalance your life so that you can live it in harmony; where your work, your play, your relationships, and your dreams come together in a balance, created with a full awareness of who YOU are and what YOU want.

And yes, want may be a four letter word, but it's not necessarily a bad one. There is nothing wrong with wanting things. There is nothing wrong with wanting your life to be filled with beautiful art and music. There is nothing wrong with wanting beautiful clothes, or a house on a lovely hill, or desiring a job that is fulfilling and pays you well. There is something wrong with wanting things just for the sake of having them, or with coveting the possessions that others have. The reason is simple. Wanting to fulfill your own destiny and attain your own Simple Truth is very different than pursuing a self-destructive path by trying to live by the expectations that others have for you.

Instead of running away from the world around you, stake a claim in the world you now live in. Take a pre-trip look into your baggage and start identifying the old things that no longer apply to your life. Once you know what's in them, it's okay to move your bags into a closet, so that you can unpack them at a later time. Use the empty space that's left behind to sit and start meditating. You will see that you already know what you want in your baggage and what needs to be dealt with. It's just a matter of finding your own center from which to deal with it.

Stay on Track to Your Simple Truth

Shortly before my father passed away he came up to New York for a weekend of sailing. I had called him the weekend before that the engine on our boat had conked out, but we both laughed and decided to go for it anyway. After all, we reasoned, sailboats had sailed for centuries without motors. That is what they are built for. So, after a lengthy train ride, we raised our canvas and edged away from our mooring. For the next four days we were at the mercy of the wind and the tide.

On the first day we made fairly good headway and dropped anchor in a cove called Cold Spring Harbor. We congratulated ourselves on our success at not having an engine and went to bed after a dinner of fish stew.

On the second day we had light winds and spent several hours just bobbing around. We laughed at our lack of progress and worked hard to eke out what little leeway we could from the light, and sometimes non-existent, breeze. We had some near calamities with passing barges. But in the end it was one of the most magical sailing adventures of my life.

During one of the lulls I had gotten frustrated with our lack of progress and was busy myself adjusting the various lines in an effort to get us going when my father asked what I was doing. I told him I was trying to get a bit more speed. To which he smiled and said "to go where?" I stammered because we really had no destination in mind. "Come back here and take a seat," he said.

"There are going to be a lot of times in your life when you're not going to have any control over your circumstances. You cannot do anything about the wind or the tides. So why not just enjoy the ride? Why not focus on the things where you can make a difference in your life?" He said. "The rest has a way of working itself out in the end."

What I didn't know at the time was he had looked at his tape measure. He had less than a year left in his life at this point. He knew it. He also knew that reaching a new harbor would not make a difference in either of our lives. But having a long weekend together would. And it has. The last conversations we had that weekend remain some of the most powerful memories I have to this day. They always will.

It is why it is so important to always keep in mind what is truly important in life. You will stray, you will get distracted. But don't let that frustrate you. Simply remember to return to the present time and remember to focus on the things that will matter the most over the long haul that is your life.

Make a conscious decision to live YOUR life. Know that the events of the world will make it difficult from time to time to do so. But just resolve to return to YOUR own Simple Truth. That is the best way to make it all that you can. It's the only life you have at this time. Regardless of what comes next, why waste a precious second of it on anything?

An Exercise – Follow Your Dreams

The key to happiness is to find your own Simple Truth and to follow it. Your Simple Truth is your guidepost to enable you to direct yourself through the choices and decisions that will forever shape your life and your happiness. So try this simple exercise the next time you find yourself wondering who you are or what you want. It is a way to find, and re-find, your Simple Truth no matter where your path leads.

Set aside half an hour. Take out a piece of paper and write down the name of a recent purchase you made. Now write down the reason you purchased it. Just below that, write down the reason why you did what you did. Be honest, because there is no one else that will hear your rationale. The only rule is, do not look into the past for a reason. Only look forward and into the future. If you just broke up with someone it may sound something like this:

> I just rented a new home.
> "Why?"
> I did it because I need a new place to live.
> "Why?"
> Because I want to start having people over and entertaining, and my old home doesn't show off the real me.

"Why?"
Because I want to start my life again without a shadow hanging over me.
"Why?"
Because I feel like there is a whole new world filled with new people to meet.
"Why?"
Because I want to live my way.
"Why?"
Because a new life will make me happy.

You will notice two things. First, the future is a lot brighter if you don't look back. Second, all of your decisions ultimately lead to your wanting to be happy. Try this with any number of your decisions. Work through them without dwelling on something in the past. Instead think how your decision will affect the future.

If you can apply this exercise to your future decisions, the world will become a happier, more pleasant place that supports your Simple Truth, and your happiness.

An Exercise – Create a Visualization Collage

If a picture is worth a thousand words then a self portrait is priceless. Even if you cannot paint, sketch, photograph or draw, there is a way for you to create an image of who you are that will grow and evolve as you do. It is called a Visualization Collage

A visualization collage is a collection of images, thoughts and ideas that you associate with. It is used by art therapists because a collage is a very forgiving medium. I have been keeping an ongoing collage for close to fifteen or twenty years. It is made up of layer upon layer of postcards, magazine images, notes and writings.

I use it to inspire me, to look for ideas, and to remember what is important, painful, wonderful and unimportant as I grow and as my collage changes. My collage includes photos of East Asian furniture that I think is beautiful, a photo of a Cucuteni Venus Figurine from E900 B.C., quotes, a scrap of paper with the words "You are not what you do, you are how you do it," a sailboat crashing through the waves, the constellation Orion, the image of a man alone, the image of a couple hugging. Each of those images calls to mind something from my past, present and future.

Therapists sometimes call this type of collage a projective technique. In plain English that is a technique used to get an individual to tell a story. We are doing the same thing, only you are telling yourself your story.

Start by collecting images that jump out at you as you read a magazine. Do not try to control or select the images based on what you want or need. Instead, select an image that moves you or stirs a change in you. Do not worry about why, the fact that it does is enough.

It could be an image of a dream home you cherish. It could be an image of a model you think is attractive. It could be the image of a landscape or a photo that takes your breath away. Do not worry about why. Just start the process of collecting images, quotes, even your own notes about you.

As your collage grows, spend a little time looking at an image and ask yourself why you picked it. Perhaps it reminded you of a place you visited or want to visit. If so, ask yourself why? If it is a photo of a beautiful model, ask yourself what you specifically liked about the person in the photo. Perhaps it is the curve of a chin, the shape of a hip. If it is a home, ask yourself why you like the architecture or the décor.

Use the images as a way to compartmentalize your own thoughts, fears, wants and dreams. Use it as a way to safely open the boxes that each image, quote or idea represents. In time you may look at an image and find it is no longer relevant. You may see shifts in the type of images that jump out at you. Note these, as well as the changes that occur within you.

Remember, this is a visualization of what is important to you, not an image of YOU. Use it as a tool to guide your personal evolution and as a way to observe and shape your growth.

Step 4:

Replace Your Old Programs

Peel Your Layers to Expose Your Core

You have no doubt heard the acorn and oak analogy before. The acorn provides the potential for what the tree can become. But the environment that the tree grows in is what forms the oak that you see. Throughout its life the genetic material from the seed doesn't change. But the mature trees vary wildly from the resulting wind and rain, the altitude and environment it grew up in. An acorn that was planted in a city park grows to be a different tree than one that grew from an acorn planted in the wilds of New Hampshire or even in the mountains of Colorado.

Had the same seed ended up on the rocky coast of Maine it would have been gnarled and stunted by the salt air and Nor' Easters. Had it been planted in Napa Valley it would look like a different tree than one that was planted in the middle of Manhattan's Central Park.

No matter where that acorn ends up, it still ends up being a beautiful tree, but its beauty will be shaped by its environment. The branches still fill out with green leaves that reach for the energy of the sun. The roots dig deep into the ground in search of water and to support its growth. The trunk and bark grow to be resilient to the world around it, complete with broken limbs and gnarled knots as proof of its struggle with the elements.

Taken on their own each of these blemishes might be considered an imperfection, the result of some minor mishap or near catastrophe that the tree survived. But together, they show the life of the tree. Together these imperfections are signs of the tree's life and experience and true beauty. Individually they may appear to be faults, but taken together, each adds character and makes the tree unique.

The same is true for you. When you were born you were born with YOUR own Simple Truth. That Truth was, and still is, the seed to who you are and who you can be. It includes your genetic coding as well as the mental and spiritual fingerprints that remain a part of you today. Your Simple Truth is a roadmap that defines the basis for your personality, your capabilities and your inclinations. Some of you were born with the potential for engineering genius, others for athletic greatness. Some of you were born with a creative ability for self discovery and expression that others just don't have. Some of you were born with genetic aberrations that reflect in our physical capabilities or our state of mind. The reality is there is nothing you can do about what you were born with. All you can do is find out what your own Simple Truth is and then work 110% to make the most of what you were given.

The lessons you have learned and the experiences you have lived through are what make you who you are today. The scars that you worry have damaged you are what make you unique and interesting. They make you stand out.

Yes, life is about surviving. But it is also about living and learning. It is about adapting and growing. It is about experiencing the downs as well as the ups. These are the things that have helped you to grow into the person you are today. They will continue to help you grow into the person you want to be tomorrow; all within the parameters that were coded into that original seed you were born from. Getting back to the essence of that seed is what this part is all about, by unpeeling the layers that cover the essence of who you are.

Unpeeling your layers is not the same as getting rid of them. Instead, it means to become aware of them and acknowledge them without judging yourself or anyone else along the way. You don't want to lose the experiences that make you who you are today, even if you think they are imperfections. Every one of those is an important part of you. The loss of which would diminish the essence of who you are, and that would be tragic. As traumatic as your bad experiences may have been, they are still a very real part of you. They help to define you, and will continue to do so for the rest of your life. As important you do not want to have to repeat them. In that sense, none of your experiences are truly bad. They are all lessons and are now an essential part of who you are.

What you can do is recognize them and understand them for what they are. You can also determine what part they will play in your life from this point onward. After all, it is your life. While you cannot control the world around you, you do have control over how you respond to it and how you allow your experiences to shape your life. You can choose how you define your relationship with the events in your past and determine what part it will play in your life from this point forward.

Know that your past life will influence your future, but it does not have to dictate your actions moving forward. Only you can dictate that.

Find Your Layers

The vast majority of us were born with a mix of physical, mental and metaphysical traits that make up each of our Simple Truths. No matter what you were given, each of you has gone through a process of discovery that is called life. This process led you to learn the truths of the physical as you learned to survive and evolve. Life also enabled you to learn the truths, what was acceptable and unacceptable, of whatever society you were raised in. You will notice that as you grew your education went from broad to specific. Once you learn how to breathe and nourish yourself, you then learned how to find the food you enjoyed and avoid the food you didn't. In the beginning you learned how to live within society's rules, before you learned the rules of whatever clique or group you associated with. Now it is time to live with your own rules.

Your progress has gone something like this:

The Physical World you had to learn survive in the physical world and acquire the basic elements to live

The Social World you had to learn from others so that you could live with others, grow and prosper

Your Personal World you have to learn who you are and to focus your growth on the lessons you were meant to learn

When you were born into the world you were completely unaware. You had no defenses and no roadmap. You did what humans have done for eons, you learned from the advice and experiences of those around you. At first you relied on your parents for their protection and their guidance. They did their best to teach you how to stay safe and avoid the pitfalls of the world.

As you matured you relied on others who you thought were smarter and more experienced to guide you. You reached out to others, observing what they did and asking questions so that you could learn, grow and evolve. As you did your world expanded. But the people who taught you also influenced you. They influenced your thinking and taught you biases that you were not born with. They added layers onto your core.

Perhaps your brothers or sisters gave you advice. Maybe it didn't come across in plain English, but in the smaller comments they made about how you looked or acted. Perhaps your parents didn't just tell you what was edible, but guided you on how to eat properly. They looked down on your behavior if it wasn't to their standards. Maybe your classmates said things that you responded to in order to fit in. Maybe you added to the layers of others as you tried to teach them what you knew. You weren't intentionally trying to keep others in line. But that's what happens.

Some of these lessons were given innocently enough. Some of them were done out of anger. Most were probably not verbal, but took the form of sneers, sideways stares or looks of disdain. They could have been off the cuff comments or made in the heat of the moment. They could have been made with the best of intentions or with the worst. What was said doesn't matter. Because all kinds of things are said when everyone's trying to figure out how the world works. What is important is how each of us held onto them and what level of importance you still place on them.

The vast majority of these "comments" were not meant to stay with you for as long as they have, but they did. Some you may realize are there. Others you may not even know exist. But there they are and they continue to have a deep effect on your life because you continue to empower them. You enable them because you have grown used to having them there. It has become easier for you to keep running on your treadmill, than to step off and relearn what you already know deep down inside.

> ***Simple Truth***
>
> *There is always an intent working behind the scenes, whether you are aware of it or not.*

The layers that now control your life are less like the rings of an onion or an oak tree, which show successive layers of growth. They are more like layers of dark, sticky tar that have been splashed onto your core. They cover the true YOU, and create the surface that everyone knows you to be. The you that everyone knows is a combination of YOU, but also all of the self-doubt and insecurities, the self-loathing and fear that hold you back from being the person you were born to be. Remove these layers and you can be the person you should be, the person you want to be, based on your own Simple Truth.

While others can create they layers, you are the only one who can give them the power they hold over your life. You do this because of your 40,000 year old programming. You remember the bad memories more often than good ones because they are part of your survival programming. You learned how to eat and drink based on avoiding foods you didn't like. You learned how to avoid physical harm by staying out of the way of certain people. Then you learned how to avoid emotional harm by putting up your own self-protective walls.

As you grew, you tested the world carefully by joining social clubs, sororities and fraternities that you felt comfortable with. You avoided the pain of rejection by staying away from people that challenged you or didn't agree with you. There is nothing wrong with this. These patterns are part of human evolution. They are part of the greatest evolutionary advantage that the human species had – our desire to bond together into like-minded groups and societies. The desire for kinship enabled our ancestors to work together and hunt beasts far larger than they were. It enabled them to work together to build houses, towns, and cities. It still does. But in the modern world of machines and automation, it also traps us, not by the need to survive, but by our innate desire to do what society demands of us.

When you were young, your need to be a part of the group helped you to survive and avoid the mistakes others had made. Your own painful memories kept you from repeating your own past mistakes. But, now that you have grown, those survival traits will now limit your personal growth unless you learn to manage them.

Yes you are programmed to avoid mistakes. We all are. But there is a tremendous difference between a yellow light and a red light at an intersection. One is a sign for caution. The other is a signal to completely stop. While the bad memory of an old breakup should be a warning light for future relationships, it should not, in and of itself, dictate who you trust or how you should live your life.

This is why it is so important to acknowledge the layers you have held onto and why it is so important to not remove them altogether. You want to be able to use them so that you can make good choices in the future and put a smart "a", for "action" into Living Your Life with CaRE.

Follow Your Triggers

We all have triggers that set us off. Somebody makes a comment and our emotions start to boil. Or somebody makes a gesture and you think they're giving you "attitude," one of those wonderful words that mean everything and nothing these days.

Simple Truth

The one that angers you controls you. Don't give anyone that power, especially if they do it intentionally.

Rarely are these reactions warranted. More often than not, they are over-reactions based on the memories you're carrying of old events that happened long before. While your conscious mind may be aware of what you think are the facts at hand, your subconscious mind is relating them to layers you covered over long ago. You may have thought the slights of your past were long forgotten, but they are still there, deep inside of you.

In the West they are sometimes called Latent Memories. In the East they are often referred to as Energy Blockages. No matter what words you prefer to use, each refers to unresolved issues. The best way to free yourself from the agitation and anxiousness, as well as the fear and self-loathing that they can bring is to identify what they are and remove them at their root. This is the point where the latent memories or the blockages first created the layer that is now driving your response.

You can do this in much the same way that you remove a virus from your computer. When you have a virus on your computer, you first look at the effect it is having on your system. Then you take the time to identify the side effects it is having so that you can locate it in your root directory. While you're there you look to see what else the virus is doing and what havoc it is wreaking on your system. After you've found it and isolated it, only then can you prevent it from doing any more harm.

The same is true for your own personal operating system. Take a moment to look back at your life. Don't go back too far. Simply find several recent events that caused your emotions to suddenly soar or caused you to act out. Don't worry about the outcome or how you handled them. Simply be aware of the times when your blood pressure shot up, or you spun out of control, or you found yourself instantly smitten with someone by just a look. Sit by yourself and review these events as dispassionately as you can.

The entire episode could have started with a comment that someone made. It could have been the sudden anger you felt when a car cut you off this morning or a burst of envy you felt when someone walked into the gym or yoga studio where you work out. For now, simply write down the event and what your resulting emotion was. Don't bother to write down the details of what happened yet.

I often find it is easier to start with a pleasant event. For instance, have you ever smelled the scent of coffee in the morning and suddenly felt comforted? Coffee does not have a secret ingredient that brings a feeling of comfort. It is triggering a memory of some wonderful event that gave you comfort. Perhaps it was watching your mother making coffee for your father and evoked the love they felt for each other. Or perhaps it was the camaraderie and sense of belonging you felt while talking with other people as you waited in line before starting your day.

Write a pleasant trigger down and trace its path to such an event to learn how the process works.

For instance:

> I recently passed a small pub while walking home from a long day at work in Manhattan. The sounds coming from the open door caused me to smile. I had not been there in years. I could not help myself as I stuck my head inside to see if it was still the same. It was. The last time I had been there was years before on a cold wintry day with my wife and her family. It was a blizzard outside and the pub had a roaring fire. We spent hours in there talking, laughing and bonding. It was a magical afternoon, all of which came back to me and made me smile on this warm summer night. Those memories were so powerful I could not help but feel warmer inside. The joy was so great it changed my entire evening.

That was a positive trigger and a wonderful example of how a simple memory can take hold of you. It can take over your entire day before you ever have a chance to consider if the direction it's taking you on is the way you want your day to unfold. If this is how a good memory can affect my day, imagine how a bad memory can do the same in the opposite direction. If you allow it to grab a hold of you, it will pull upon memories you didn't even know you had, and before you know it your entire day will be in the hands of a memory from years ago. My experience was an easy layer to decipher. It was pleasant and light. It was positive so I let it in and allowed it to embrace me.

On the other side, have you ever walked into a business meeting and felt outclassed and incompetent? Have you ever waited for a date who was running late and felt completely inadequate? These are all examples of how a latent memory or an energy blockage comes out. They come out as an emotion that you're not quite sure where it comes from. A meeting alone should not instantly make you feel incompetent. A date running late should not make you feel anything less wonderful than you are. Something else is making you feel this way, and even though you can get someone to help you deal with it, only you can identify what that is.

Most of the layers that drive your life on a daily basis can be less than pleasant. Those are the survival traits that your subconscious has buried until it needs them. It is a natural reaction so that you don't have to deal with them in their entirety every time they are triggered. Instead all you feel is the residual anger, envy and fear that rise up within you.

Many of these memories have been with you for longer than you can remember. Many of them you probably don't even realize exist anymore. They are so entwined into your very being that to start unraveling them may even seem to unravel you.

So, start at the beginning. Start where you are right now. Look at one of the recent events that you wrote down that was pleasant. Think about how that event triggered an emotional reaction. It does not have to have led to an over-the-top reaction. It could be one that made you simply feel happy or content, even if you are not sure why. Perhaps somebody made a comment or gave you a look and you suddenly felt very good about yourself. Hold on to that moment and try to remember another case in your past where you had the same emotion.

This time, backtrack from your emotion to the event that triggered your response. Keep trying to think back further and further into your past for other emotions just like your current one. Write down the possible triggers to each of these events. If you can go back far enough you will start to identify the layer you are now wading through. You might not go all the way back at the point of origin for this particular event. You might just get a feeling that you're in a pool of emotion within which are floating seemingly random memories that are attached to it.

It may come to you while you are meditating. It may come to you in a dream. It doesn't happen in a day or even a week. It takes time.[10] What you will find is that once you open up an event, your brain doesn't just stop working once it has started exploring. It keeps exploring and processing in the background; sometimes only presenting you with a bit of information when you are more relaxed or able to handle it. So be aware when it does come to you and write down what you are experiencing. These notes will provide you with a roadmap of your layers.

Once you have done this, try exploring a different kind of layer. I used to get very upset when someone showed up late. If someone was even five minutes late I started to wallow in a series of emotions that went from feeling disrespected to feeling unloved to eventually wallowing in just plain old anger. When the person I was waiting for finally showed up my evening was already ruined. I got so good at wallowing in my own emotions that I could go from excited and overjoyed about the prospects of an evening to utterly miserable and self-sabotaging. All of this in just fifteen minutes. What made it worse is that I would spend the rest of the evening unconsciously trying to make my date feel just as bad as I felt.

How could I let something so out of my control – my date's timing – take such complete control of my life? The answer lay in my past. Once I started working back through my events I quickly realized that my response had nothing to do with the clock, but with my own perception of respect. I was the youngest of three boys. I was constantly struggling to not be the little one pulling up the rear. I so craved respect and so resented being left behind that it started to undermine a big part of my life. Once I understood that, once I could uproot my old program and buffer

---

[10] Exploring and dealing with your layers can sometimes be a traumatic experience. I strongly advise having a trained, accredited professional help you explore them. They can often provide insight you are simply not able to provide yourself.

it with a different perspective, the issue went away. It helped me realize this theme had been directing a major part of my life. I was making decisions for my career, not on what I actually wanted to do with my life, but based on the perceived praise I thought I would gain.

Now, I am not saying it is okay to be late. What I am saying is that by shifting your awareness from external events going on around you, to the internal triggers they touch, you can gain the happiness and self confidence that will make your life a pleasure to live. You can shift your response to the world by identifying a single issue and working back to discover the old programming and the layers that are negatively affecting how you live your life.

Along the way you will start to realize that something small, i.e., becoming angry when someone is late is actually caused by a much deeper issue, i.e., being overly sensitive to the idea of respect, which in turn was caused by a younger sibling complex that had much further reaching importance in my life. How far reaching? It caused me to make career decisions that may not have been in my best interests. It caused me to push on deals just to prove that I could. It also caused me to take on projects and clients that I really didn't want for the simple fact of boosting my bottom line.

So think back to a recent instance in which you were embarrassed, resentful, or angry. Think to a moment when you were not in control. Take the time to trace it back to similar instances in your life, to similar memories. Try to remember how those instances are connected to other parts of your life. Take your time. This is an ongoing process that comes through in the revelations and interconnections that bubble up as you free your subconscious to reveal them when it is ready.

Peel Back Your Layers

You give memories prominence and significance by taking them seriously and giving them credence. The more seriously you take something the more important it becomes. The less serious you take something the less influence it has over your life.

For example, when you left high school you probably left many of your classmates behind. When you left an old job, you probably lost contact with many of your workmates. Even though you left them all at the same time not all of them figure as prominently in your memories. Those who you were closer to now play a larger part in your life. Those you weren't close to play a smaller part or none at all. Your memories affect your life in the same way. The more importance you place on a given memory, the larger a part it plays in your life.

This has great significance in how you should deal with them. First realize that you are in control over your memories. You have the ability to dial your memories up and dial them down. You can empower them or distance them from your life depending on how you manage your relationship with them. You don't need to remove them from your life. You couldn't even if you tried. However you can establish ground rules for them from this day forward.

Just by acknowledging that a layer exists, you are exposing it to the light; even if for a few seconds. We have all had a memory pop into our heads. But instead of dealing with it, we pack it safely into a box so that we can "deal with it later." But it doesn't go away when we do that. It stays there.

So why stop there? Go to the next level by spending some time writing about how that layer has affected your life. Don't worry about how good or how bad your grammar is. You're not doing this to get published or to win an award. You're writing to discover yourself and to see how your old layers affect the decisions you now make every day.

Start with an exercise of free association. As before, begin with a recent event. Write it down. Next, write down the emotions it brings out. Then follow one of those emotions to other events that have had the same emotional tie. Follow your memories back to the people and instances that triggered that same response in the past. Don't worry about commenting on them or trying to diagnose your own responses, merely become aware of the different instances and emotions that make up a single layer that you are carrying.

Take my example for instance. Think about how being the youngest brother in a competitive household shaped me. Maybe it caused me to strike out on my own as an act of rebellion. Maybe it caused me to be overly sensitive to a perceived lack of respect. When I started to write about how that one issue – the perceived lack of respect – shaped other decisions I started to realize how much I was living my life in response to people and events that had happened well in the past, and that I had absolutely no control over. I also realized that if I addressed my issues of perceived respect I could tear down an entire wall that I had constructed for myself out of other people's comments.

I tore down that wall, that layer, by taking two simple steps. First, I realized that nobody else made this an issue for me. I and I alone empowered my layer. I did it all by myself. Most of the comments that were made were not done maliciously. That was simply part of growing up and learning how people acted. Besides, when someone made a comment to me, I know I made the same kind of snarky, biting comments right back. So there are no innocents in the world of growing up. But that does not mean you have to keep living that way. You can grow past it.

I did it by embracing my layer. I examined each one on paper, through my writing, so that I could become fully aware of the impact they were having on me. I observed how each one affected my life and how they shaped the different choices that I made.

I then thought about how those choices created the life I was living. I looked to see how long I had been living my life in response to each layer and realized how many opportunities I had given up as a result. As I did this, it dawned on me at how ridiculous it was that I was still giving up so much of my life because of something that happened so many years ago. By trying to control my life, I had actually lost my life to the memories of something that had happened twenty or thirty years ago.

At that point I did the only thing that I could do, I laughed. I laughed at myself for giving my layers control over me. I laughed at how powerless my layers were that I once gave so much importance to. I laughed at the layers and at the power I gave them.

As ridiculous as it may sound this is exactly how to minimize your own layers; by laughing at them. Work a smile onto your face. Then laugh at how you once lived your life by someone else's idea of how you should live it. Laugh at the fact that you actually gave someone else the ability to control your life. See how ridiculous it is that someone in your past, that you may or may not even talk to any more, is still affecting your actions without even knowing it.

Once your laughter has died down to a chuckle, you will realize that it is you who not only empower your layers, but also the people around you. You cannot stop an older sister from teasing you. You cannot stop a screaming boss from screaming at you. All you can do is control how you respond to them. By not empowering them, you undermine their ability to affect your life. You also open up opportunities to change your life because it no longer seems to be such a daunting prospect.

Undermine the power your layers have by not giving them any. Take away their power by realizing how absurd it is that you have given them any power in the first place. Laugh at yourself and your layers to reduce their impact because they are no longer to be taken seriously. When you do this, open yourself up to a new way of living a lighter, happier life that realizes the folly of living in today's world with the kind of outdated programming that you have relied on, up until this moment.

It will be the breath of fresh air you have been looking for.

Replace Pain with Love

You will find that after you peel back your layers and remove your old programming, you will see that no matter what actions created it, it was more than likely filled with feelings of regret, pain, shame and anger. These are the emotions that held you back from growing and being the person you were meant to be.

When that layer is removed there will be a void, a vacuum left in its place. So what do you fill it with? The answer can be found, again, in some very old traditions and practices from around the world. Christianity, Judaism, Muslim, and Buddhism all speak of love as a powerful force. So do the infinite number of other religions, philosophies and more contemporary notables like Mahatma Gandhi and Mother Teresa.

I know it may sound like folly to some, but if you turn from anger, hate, and disgust, you open yourself up to an entire world of opportunity by responding to others and outside situations with Loving Kindness, Compassion, Joy and Equanimity.[11]

Now, I know these may sound ethereal to some, but if you can remember to respond to other people and outside stimuli with an open heart and a feeling of love, joy, compassion and equanimity, instead of your natural response of fear and anger, you can truly change your view of the world, and in so doing, the world.

Psychologists refer to this process as a method of behavior therapy called reciprocal inhibition. It is based on the fact that the human mind can only hold one thought or attitude at a time. So when you are thinking of love, your brain cannot think about hate. When you think of compassion, your brain cannot think about jealousy.

By constantly returning your brain to positive thoughts, you can train yourself how to respond to the world around you. You, in effect, inhibit the negative responses by constantly introducing positive ones.

In Sanskrit, this concept is called *pratipaksha bhavanam*, which simply means the cultivation of an opposing thought. By interruption your actions with the process of CaRE, and by introducing positive responses into your life, you can move your life to be the one you love, through the simple choices you make every day.

So just keep in mind what are known as "The Four Immeasurables" as you remove your old layers. They will help you replace your old program of fight or flight with a positive new one. They include:

---

[11] Thank you to Dr. Miles Neale for your insight and wisdom that it is not enough to peel back, but there is a need to fill up the emptiness with love.

Loving-kindness: The wish that all sentient beings, without any exception, be happy.

Compassion: The hope that a person's sufferings will diminish; "the wish for all sentient beings to be free from suffering."

Joy: Feeling joy in the accomplishments of a person — either yourself or another.

Equanimity: Learning to regard events and people around you equally, regardless of whether they are positive or negative.

The ability to achieve this calls for a level of detachment that you can realize through meditation and mindful living. By maintaining your balance, you can learn to experience your world with a clear mind, unclouded by past experiences or future aspirations, unblemished by a sense of gain or loss, a need to blame, even a sense of failure, but of acceptance.

To achieve this is to empower yourself with the ability to make the right life choices that are YOURS, not from those around you, from your past, or even from your future; but from YOU in the present.

Forgive Yourself & Move On

It may sound ridiculous that I am asking you to forgive yourself, but that is the second step you must take. I don't mean just putting on a smile, patting yourself on the back and saying "there, there." I'm talking about really looking at your life's events and seeing how they have affected you, and then letting them go in a healthy way.

When you forgive someone else you empower them with control over who you are and how you act. So before you even think about forgiving someone else, you need to first forgive yourself. You need to acknowledge that you and only you have control over your life. It is up to you if stay in a room with someone who pushes your buttons. It is up to you if you keep sitting in your boss's office as they scream, rant and rave. It is up to you if you accept a dinner invitation with someone that you really have no interest in seeing. It is your life. You and only you can keep yourself on your current path. So forgive yourself for following your human nature. Forgive yourself for blindly accepting someone else's idea of what your life should be like. Forgive yourself for making the choices you have made, and move on. Only once you have forgiven yourself, can you forgive whoever is around you honestly, truly and with compassion.

When you forgive someone else, you are giving them permission for whatever they have done. They will not, and most likely cannot, change who they are. Only you can change the events of the world, by changing how you respond to them. If you allow them to affect your moods then you are empowering them, no matter how many times or how deeply you forgive someone.

So by all means forgive someone to clear the air and reset your relationship to a neutral position. But then make sure you also reset that relationship to create one that is nurturing and positive. You need to remind yourself that it is up to you to start creating positive relationships with people that will add to your life rather than detract from it. So forgive yourself for your past mistakes, every one of us has had plenty of them. Forgive those around you for any transgression they have made. But then move forward.

Seek out and create relationships that will help you achieve whatever it is that you want from life. Instead of dating someone that makes you feel inadequate and then forgiving them for doing so, look for someone who is on a similar path and who will augment your life. Instead of following an old pattern that you know will inevitably end in the wrong place, identify the layer and the pattern in your life that is causing you to fall off your path. Then create a new pattern that will take you to the places you want to go. For some of you that might mean distancing yourself from a family member or even a friend who constantly makes you feel less than wonderful or as if you are boxed into a corner.

It may create a loss for you. That is okay. It does not have to be permanent. Once your layers are removed and old patterns are erased, you can re-establish an old relationship on new terms, with new rules and with healthy patterns.

While I cherish family above all, not every interaction with your family is a good one. While friendships should be a bond that lasts forever, not every moment will be a positive one. In many cases your own willingness to please, to avoid conflict or to "go with the flow" can undermine your own self worth and your ability to live YOUR life. So give yourself permission to evolve beyond your old life. Give yourself permission to evolve and flourish. If those people still love you for who YOU are, then they will stay with you. If not, then forgive yourself for being true to YOURSELF and move on.

If that last statement did not bring a small chuckle, then go back and re-read it. Just the idea of having to forgive yourself for being true to who YOU are is ridiculous. But that is how badly our programming is affecting every one of us every day. The very idea that you need to change who you are to fit someone else's idea of what life is, in itself, absurd. So evolve beyond where you are today. Forgive yourself for being YOURSELF and keep growing.

As for everyone around you, stop forgiving them for repeatedly stepping on your toes, and ask them to stop apologizing when they do the same. Instead, simply ask them to please not do it again. Don't let them use societal permissions like "oh, I'm just kidding," or "don't take it personally" to slide over transgressions. It is far too easy to file a comment like that into the grey area of non-action and allow the seeds of another layer to be planted by smiling, waving a hand, and saying "oh, don't worry about it."

Yes, it avoids a conflict now, but it creates a layer that will rise up later. So accept an apology once, maybe twice. But afterwards forgive yourself for being YOURSELF and ask them to not do it again. Don't let them create new layers.

See YOUR World

Each one of us lives our lives in a bubble of sorts that hardens with age. For children, whose minds are more open and accepting, the walls are porous. They experience the world with all five senses in a way that is closer to how it truly is. They have yet to form the layers that create the bias and skewed perspective that comes with age. For better or worse they have not learned the subtleties on what is proper and improper, and are often freer with their comments than the rest of us. As they age their walls will thicken and become more opaque. They start to see the world in a way that is clouded by their changing perceptions of how life should be or how others see it for them.

No matter where you are in life or where you want to go, realize that your view of the world will always be slightly tinted. It is also why it's so important to work on making the walls of your world as clear as possible if you want to evolve to the next level. Once they are clear, you can then paint them whatever color you want, but only after you come close to seeing yourself and your life in as true a form as possible.

You Relive your Past through Tinted Glasses

To some extent every memory you revisit is tinted with rose colored glasses or clouded by fog. When you look at your memories you are viewing them with eyes that have lost their objectivity. How skewed your sight is depends on the life you have led. For better or for worse, every one of us skews our memories to fit our perspective on life. An angry person sees life as a series of attacks. A loving person sees life as a series of opportunities. If you look back at a disagreement you had, there is your side, their side, and the truth to what actually happened. No matter how fair you try to be, it's almost impossible to not have some kind of bias effect your perspective. It's just the way the brain works. But you do need to be aware that somehow your memories will be slightly different from how others remember and from the reality of what actually happened.

If you were able to go back in time to revisit a cherished memory, the reality was probably not as dreamlike as you might remember it. Perhaps you remember a wonderful Bed & Breakfast where you and someone you loved spent a wonderful weekend. If that relationship blossomed into a life-long love that weekend may be viewed as perfect in every way. If not, then that may be seen more as a lost weekend where you did something with somebody not worthy of allocating a lot of brain-space to. In either case the reality is probably somewhere in between.

A slightly frayed bedcover could be seen as rustic and romantic or shoddy and beaten down. There may have been a cold fog that was either viewed as miserable and damp or romantic and secretive. Your memories are seen, not by their real colors, but by how they fit into the rest of your life.

The same is true for the way you remember the smaller events of your life and for how they crate the layers around YOU. Those that undermine your sense of self may not, in reality, be as significant as you once thought they were. If you were at a weak and vulnerable point in your life, you may have given an offhanded comment more prominence than it deserved. If you were feeling good about your life, you may not have even remembered that same comment.

It's how your brain works. It tries to optimize its space, allocating memories based on their relevance. It assumes the things that we remember when we were feeling hypersensitive were more important. Even if that hypersensitivity is long gone the layer that was created can still be there. This is why it's important to look into your past and into your layers, so that you can unpeel the ones that are no longer important.

If you call up an old classmate and ask about a comment they made years ago, I doubt they will remember it, no matter how deeply it has pained you all these years. I've tried this. Thanks to the Internet, I've connected with friends from school who I haven't spoken to in years. In every case their memory of who I was in school is very different from who I remember being; in most cases for the better. So your memories of the bad experiences in your life are just as skewed as the beautiful ones. They are all seen through the layers you have created.

Just keep that in mind as you work through your layers. They will all be skewed by your own perspective. Realize that you were never the klutz or the spurned teenager you may have thought you were. Even the football heroes and prom queens had their own insecurities that they remember far more vividly than the flashing lights and the headlines in the school newspaper that the rest of the school saw around them.

Choose which memories to hold on to.

Just as you skew how you see a memory, you also prioritize the importance of the memories that you hold onto. You choose to remember certain components of a memory more than others. Which, in and of itself is not bad; unless that is you continue to reinforce your own insecurities by your own self selectivity.

The choice as to which memories you hold on to is entirely your own. It may not be easy, but in the end, you and only you can decide how you view life. It's like deciding which movie ticket to buy. You can see a scary movie, a blissfully wonderful movie, or a true-to-life documentary. All depending on what ticket you decide to buy.

Think back to your own high school days. Remember that tall girl who dressed perfectly? The one who always knew what the celebrities were doing and always seemed to be just one step ahead? She always had that poker face of bravado no matter what happened. In realty she held her cards tightly to her chest because she was afraid someone would see behind her façade. She learned early on that she could protect herself by putting up walls rather than by opening herself up. Yet what you remember is her perfection and her cutting comments that pushed you away.

What you chose to overlook in your memories were her panicked looks when she was not in control. Her quick exits when someone undermined her authority. If you look back without coloring your memories, you would see that her comments and sneers were just her way of protecting herself. She made so many of them she probably doesn't even remember any of them today. She only remembers how afraid she was of letting her guard down. Just like her, you no longer remember all of her comments, only the one or two that you allowed your own insecurities to take to heart.

We all do this. Rather than store every memory and every event that ever happened, you select what you remember in order to save brain space. You tend to forget the comments and asides that didn't matter at the time, but obsess about the comments and asides that seemed important.

You gave most of your memories importance because they struck a nerve or hit a weakness in your personality, even if they are no longer relevant. So today, even though you are a very different person than you were, you tend to remember yourself based on your hyper-sensitivities of the past.

Perhaps you were sensitive about your weight. So instead of remembering all the fun you had, you prioritized the events of your youth that dealt with weight or body image. Perhaps you obsessed about your inability to quickly remember dates and facts. So instead of remembering the day you got an answer right, or the day you looked great in school, or the day you felt great about yourself, you remember the one time you messed up on a pop quiz in history class.

Perhaps the sting of that event caused you to hide when your future teachers asked about math equations, dates or history. While you had many great qualities this became the fault that you obsessed over for years to come. So rather than spending your time focusing on what you were good at, you became increasingly sensitive to a perfectly natural inability to remember dates. Rather than simply admitting this was not your strong-suit and working to improve it you clung to that one fault and started to build your own layer. You became hyper-aware every time you missed a question about dates. Maybe you even start to avoid history class altogether.

You never paid much attention to the fact that you were voted class philosopher or threw some fantastic parties. You overlooked your "gift of gab" as something that everyone had and viewed it as nothing special. As you went through life, your layer thickened. Not because people targeted your inability to remember dates, but because you placed greater and greater emphasis on the lack of memorization that you were already sensitive toward.

So here you are, twenty years after graduating college. You have grown to be a successful sales executive. Your clients love working with you. You are making a sales presentation for a new business account, which your boss has placed an inordinate amount of pressure on to win, and you get a date in your client's history wrong. The client corrects you without really thinking too much about it. Nobody other than you even gives it a second thought because it really wasn't that important to them. You put on a smile and keep going. But inside you start to rush to finish. For some unknown reason you just want to get out of there. Your focus is no longer on the presentation but on getting out. Your energy starts to fade. You seem to lose your wind and suddenly the meeting's momentum slows down. And you are not sure why it all fell apart.

Whether the meeting was a success or a failure is not important. What is important is that a series of outdated and biased memories is controlling your life. Instead of remembering the positive side of your past, like how great you always were in social situations, or how you led your debating team, you remembered snapshots that were skewed by your own sensitivities. They were layered over and hiding your natural ability to sell. Even though your skill with dates was not what the client was looking to you for, it undermined your ability to act.

Some call it self-sabotage. Some call it choking. It is merely you clinging on to a memory, an energy block that matters to no one else but you. This is why it is so important to understand that you create your own history by choosing what you remember. On the up side, this also means that you can change your life by changing which details you emphasize about what happened. In so doing, you can remove the layers that skew how you view your past and how you will live your future.

People Hiding Their Insecurities Created Yours

Remember that guy in high school who wore his varsity jacket everywhere? He walked with a swagger and made sure everyone around him knew about his last game? You thought he had everything under control. Maybe you still do. Well, he didn't. He was just as scared and searching as you were. He just found a way to hide his own insecurities beneath his felt and leather jacket with a Varsity "V" on it. It was his way of turning the magnifying glass away from him and on to someone else, anyone else for that matter. People like that are very good at controlling their world. But they control it at the expense of those around them, and inevitably at the expense of their own personal growth.

This may sound trite, but believe it or not, you are perfect at your core. You have talents and a perspective of the world that no one else has. You just did what we all do in life. You let your programming run your life. That means you listened to other people without questioning what they were saying. So, instead of editing out the bad advice or ignoring the destructive insights, you took in the bad as well as the good. Some of it was well intentioned, but much of it from people seeking to cover up their own insecurities instead of having your best interests in mind.

This is the cycle of growing up. You seek advice when you're vulnerable. But that is exactly one point where you don't have the wherewithal to edit the advice that is given. So instead of just getting facts that will help you overcome, you also get opinions that add to your layers and strengthen the insecurities that you already have.

Even if you're not actively seeking advice, your mind is absorbing the sights and sounds of the world you live in. You cannot help but take in the comments, asides and looks that may not even be directed at you, naturally keeping the elements that you are already sensitive toward. Instead of seeing those comments as irrelevant, or as someone else's efforts at self-protection, you may instinctively apply your own fears, concerns and layers to them as if they were.

So the next time you look into your past, instead of seeing the comments that you remember as fact, start to ask yourself what else was going on at the time or with this person. Put the comments in context by asking yourself what else was happening to this person that made them lash out? What was going on with you that made you hold on to that memory? Because behind that is a key to unpeeling your layer.

You also need to look at your present life in the same way. Don't just take a comment or action at face value. Be aware and mindful so that you can look deeper and find out why someone made a comment, or why you even acknowledged it before deciding if it holds merit.

Remember, you cannot change other people. They are who they are. You can only evolve by revising how you think, act and live in the world around you.

Pare Down Your Life to Your Simple Truth

Just like internal layers that prevent you from being YOU, you also have external layers that you build up all on your own. These are created by the objects you collect and the things you hold dear. Some bring you happiness and joy, others cause remorse and pain. The first can be a house that provides you shelter from the rain or a gift that brings you wonderful memories. The second can be a mansion that has you wracked with debt or an heirloom that reminds you of an overbearing parent. The first can include a job that you enjoy even though it will never make you a millionaire. The second can be a job that will set you up for retirement even though it will create forty years of misery before you get there.

Whether an object is good or bad is different for everyone. It depends less on the object itself and more on your relationship with it, and on what kind of energy and power you give to it. In a way, it truly is the thought that counts.

If you dote on an object and rely on it for the feeling it gives you, then at some point it starts to own you, rather than the other way around. It's like the woman who owns a fabulous Chanel coat, but would never think of wearing it unless she was going to the right event. Or the man who owns a classic motorcycle but never takes it out for fear that it will get dirty. At some point these objects start to dictate how different people live their lives, rather than augmenting the lives they are already living.

If you look around your home, you have imbued every object around you with energy. Some carry a good energy that just makes you happy. Others bring sadness or the memory of a love lost that can bring you down. As with everything the memories and power an object carries changes with time. A rock that you collected on a beachside vacation can sit beautifully on your desk for years before its power changes and it becomes just one in a pile of rocks. The room that your child grew up in can be a very happy place that keeps wonderful energy for years and years. Yet after they have moved out and moved on, the energy it holds can evoke feelings of loss and loneliness. Some people can appreciate a luxury handbag based on the craftsmanship and beauty its makers gave it. If they lost the handbag, they would be sad, but it wouldn't ruin their lives. Others covet the same item because they think it will elevate their status and make them feel better about themselves. If they lost their handbag they would lose a bit of themselves with it.

The Simple Truth is everything has value beyond its price tag. That value changes based on the memories and meaning it carries for you. That value also changes with time. Which is why paring down is a healthy and ongoing activity if you want to live YOUR life and find YOUR own happiness.

My wife and I had a pile of rocks that we had collected over the years from different vacations and travels and escapes. Looking at them just made us happy. They had this joyous energy of far-away beaches and wonderful weekends.

At one point, the pile simply got too large. It started taking up room that we wanted to use for books and new found treasures. It's not that we didn't like the rocks. We simply had too many of them. So one Saturday night we went through all of the rocks and selected a few that represented the entire pile. We transferred the energy from the entire pile into just a few representational rocks. We then rode our bikes down to the Hudson River and created our own ceremony by throwing the remaining rocks into the river one by one. In effect returning each to the waters from which we took them.

The rocks were not what made us happy. The power and the memories we gave to them did. We now have a small pile of rocks that bring us a lot of happiness and make us smile every time we pass it. We also have room for new treasures that bring us even more joy and happiness than we had before.

There are two components to living YOUR life in a healthy and happy way. The first is being aware of whom you are and knowing what is important to you. The second lies in creating a supportive environment around you. No, you cannot control the world around you. But you can be responsible in how you treat it and how you allow it to treat you.

If you have a problem with alcohol, living your life with a well stocked bar is probably not the best idea. If you have an allergy to cat hair, having a cat for a pet would probably not make you happy. There is a certain level of responsibility you have to take in the friends you hold on to, the food you eat and the objects you surround yourself with. Being careful to live a life of moderation in all things will help you create an environment that lets you be YOU. After all, why would you live in a home filled with memories that weigh you down? Why would you stay with people who undermine your efforts to grow? Why not create an environment, within reason, that supports your own Simple Truth and the person you want to be?

So ask yourself, what is it that you really want? Not just for today or tomorrow, but for all eternity? Is it to be happy? Is it to follow your heart? Or is it to collect objects and memorabilia? If it is to be happy, then why not do it? Now that you have started to work through your layers and taken the first steps to remove those layers that carry the most pain, why not do the same thing with the world around you?

Most people have far more than they actually need to live their lives. Most people cling to things that bring them more pain than joy. It sounds ridiculous that they do this at all, but old habits are powerful things.

How many of you hold on to an old item just because you have done so all of your life? Do you keep old clothing that you have not worn in years "just in case" there may be a costume party? Do you keep an old hammer "just in case" there is a job that you do not want to ruin your new hammer on? Do you keep a broken bicycle because you are going to fix it "one of these days?" Well, today is one of these days. Today you're going to use those items to make you feel happy, light and free.

Each and every one of the objects you are holding on to carries a lifetime worth of memories and energy with it. That is the energy you wake up to every day and go to sleep with every night. So ask yourself, is that really the kind of environment you want to live in? Is that really the kind of energy you want to live inside of? Do you want to live in the past, or in the present?

Every one of you can live with less than you have. If some calamity befell you, you might surprise yourself at how little you can actually live on. If you doubt this, just look at how people live in developing nations or in third world countries. I am not saying that is how you want to live, but I am saying that the act of living is possible with very little. More to the point, anything above the bare essentials are either comforts or luxuries.

Some of the things that you possess make life easier. Others may not be functional, but bring you happiness. Still others bring you pain because of the financial or emotional debt you incur in order to have them. I can already guess that much of what you have is not quite what you want, and are causing more problems than they are resolving.

My wife and I have a small sailboat that we use in the summers. It is not very large, but it is perfect for the two of us. We drop anchor near the shores of Long Island Sound, Peconic

Bay, or off of Shelter or Block Islands and spend our weekends reading, playing music or just watching the stars circle overhead. The cabin has the bare essentials: a bed, a stove, an old fashioned ice box. We have books and a radio, a fishing pole that still brings us dinner from time to time. It is a constant reminder of just how little we need to not only survive, but to live a wonderful life. To us anything beyond that small 250 square foot cabin is a land-locked luxury.

When people are evacuated after a disaster strikes, they are often given fifteen minutes to return to their homes and take what possessions they can carry. Rarely do people take their televisions or DVD players with them. More often they take sentimental objects that have little or no monetary value, but have an incredible amount of energy. Apparently the energy they carry is more important than the cost of the flat screen television they left behind. That should tell you something.

So look around. Think about what you would take with you if you were given fifteen minutes to evacuate. Now look at everything else you have in your possession. What would you keep if you only had 250 or 300 square feet of space to live in?

Some religions and philosophies say that ownership of anything causes pain. In the purest sense of the word, they are right. Everything does cause pain eventually, and if your goal were to live a life of absolute purity you should get rid of all your earthly belongings in order to free yourself. However, we do not live in a world of absolutes. We live in a world of trade-offs. You need shelter, food and water in order to survive. In our society those things are paid for with money that you receive by working. Nobody is disputing the fact that you need to perform some work, whether it is sweeping out an ashram for an evening meal or running a business that employs dozens of people, in order to survive. Whether it is right or wrong, that is part of the modern condition.

The question is not should you work, but what is your relationship with your work and the objects around you. Are you in control of the objects you have around you, or are they controlling how you live your life? If you have to take on additional debt just in order to have a second bedroom, if you find yourself hoarding old memorabilia because it gives you a sense of security, then you are paying a cost – financially, emotionally, or spiritually – that is preventing you from being YOU.

Beyond the basic things you need in order to survive, there are some objects that offer you comfort and well being. They either make your life easier or they give you a sense of well being. It is up to you, and only you, to decide which category an object falls into.

The over-riding rule to keep in mind is do you control the object, or does the object control you? Do you have a car that fits into your finances? Do you have a car that you can park and not worry about getting scratched? Can you afford to lose your handbag and not bemoan its loss? If you were to lose your home, would you be able to take out everything that was important to you in fifteen minutes? If not, you may need to rethink what you have.

For instance, shelter can be basic home, an apartment, or even a tent. But at what point does it start being a statement about who you are? At what point does owning a specific home become about more than just protecting yourself from the elements? We should all take pride in our homes and in the things we have worked for. But when the items you have begin to define you that is the point where you start to lose the battle. That is the point where you no longer own, but are owned by the things around you. Only you can know that point. But if you would be embarrassed having people over to a smaller home, even if it were kept as nice and orderly as your current one, then it is time to rethink the concept of ownership and property.

Think of it this way. A comfort helps you live YOUR life in an easier way. But a luxury starts to define YOUR life by adding a certain level of burden to acquire it. Comforts help you attain your goals. Luxuries cause you to change your life. Air conditioning is a comfort. Central air conditioning that puts out more BTUs than you need is a luxury. A stove to cook a meal is a comfort. A brand name stove with eight burners is a luxury. A bag to carry your essentials could be a necessity, while a designer handbag that retails for $2,500 is a luxury.

Only you can know which is which.

Exercise – Redefine What You Have

There is a fine line between appreciating clothes and art for the sake of their beauty and meaning, and wanting them because of the status you think they bestow upon you. This line is different for everyone. However, it is one of the most important lines you will discover for yourself. One that you, and only you, will ever know exists.

Take a look at the objects around you. Start a list of these items, ranking each by how important they are to you. Take your time, start with the most important and work from there.

It's okay if you're having trouble determining which is the most important. The order matters less than the exercise. Look to see which have been placed in a position of prominence and which are hidden away. You may be surprised at how you have subconsciously moved things without even thinking about it.

Next to each item, write down one of four categories that it will fit into. Everything you possess will fit into one of four categories:

Items that are essential to your life –basic shelter, food, and water

Items that add comfort to your life – car, duvet, air conditioning

Items are empowered with memories – heirloom watch, photos, even rocks

Items that are luxuries for your lifestyle – designer handbags, shoes, a luxury car or home

What you will notice from this list is that the less essential an item is, the greater the chance it will have to undermine your well being. For instance, we all need some form of food, shelter, water and clothing in order to survive. But how big of a shelter do you need? For some it is a tent. For others it may be a cabin. Still others feel the need to have a home with several bedrooms, an entertainment center, or a private swimming pool.

We can all admit that basic shelter is essential to your well being, but anything more than that falls into a grey area that only you can see through. There are comforts that you think you need, but are not truly essential to your life.

Now, put a check by the items that are luxuries. Ask yourself can you enjoy them without attachment, or do they cost you more than the benefits they provide? Does the opinion you have of yourself depend on the things you own? Do you work harder than you want to in order to maintain the lifestyle you have created for yourself?

If so, you may want to rethink your lifestyle. If it is dependent upon the objects around you, you will never truly enjoy your life. Because as soon as you attain something that you think will make you happy, you will already have your eye on the next thing you need to acquire.

At some point an item becomes more than just a comfort that helps you live a better life. When you give up the dreams and ideals that are important to you, when you start to think less of yourself and more of a brand, when you put yourself in debt or at risk in order to gain something, then the object of your desire has taken ownership of you and it's well past time to pare down.

As you go down your list ask yourself if you have used an item the past three months? If you lost it, would you be able to make do? Does it make you feel proud to own something? Does it make you wish you had something better? Do you need it, or do you simply enjoy using it?

Exercise – Find Your Triggers

Recognizing and identifying your layers is a one of the first steps to living by your Simple Truths. If you can uncover the layers that have formed over time, you can reduce their impact and start to change the way you respond to the world around you.

During your day, start to be aware of radical emotional changes as they happen. This can range from an uncontrollable fear that overtakes you, self-doubt and a feeling of failure, a feeling of being a child or a teenager who is not up to the level of those around you. It can be a sudden disgust at someone else, anger or envy.

These kinds of emotions signal that something in the world around you has triggered a response from deep within you. Even if you don't recognize the trigger, realize that you reacted to something not only in your world, but within yourself.

Make a note of the events that just happened around you. Was it the way someone spoke to you? Was it a sideways look that set you off? Do not look too deeply, but make a note of what it was.

When you have time, go back to this event and try to think back to other times when you experienced the same emotion or response. Think about what occurred just before each exchange and look for similarities. Even if you can't find a rational reason for why you responded as you did, look for the emotion and follow that.

I say this because we are all very good at creating a reason for why we did what we did, but that is not what you should be interested in. You should be interested in the emotional triggers that caused your response. And in the automatic mechanism that made you respond as you did, rather than the rationale your brain came up with to justify it later.

As you walk through this exercise make sure that you:

Remain aware of your state of mind and take note when you started to become emotional. You can use this in the future as a kind of early warning system.

Pause until you are in a neutral environment so that you can review from a dispassionate place of being.

Look back at your life and identify other instances when that same emotion arose and, as best you can, remember the events surrounding it. Realize how big a part this layer has played in your life.

Identify the overriding emotion you were feeling and start to peel back your layer, by following that emotion to an early event that may have created it without you being aware it was there?

If it was shame, were there people or events in your past that you are ashamed of? If it is guilt, did you do things that you're still guilty of?

Now comes the hard part. Write them down. Write down the events that caused these emotions. Write down your own emotions from way back when. Expose the early actions that created these layers as a personal confessional to bring them into the light so that they no longer cover all that YOU are, and all that you can be.

This is not always easy, but there is a power to the written word that brings your imagined pain into the real world. Only then can you begin to realize how much a part some small, or not so small, incident in your past is effecting your present. Only then can you confront it for what it is and start living your life with CaRE.

Live with CaRE

CaRE is not just a way to stay on your path. It is a way to make good choices throughout your life. Living with CaRE can help you gain the things that will make you happy and avoid the things that will cause you pain. No matter what your goals or objectives are in life, Living with CaRE can help you live with more focus, can help you achieve those things that are important to you, and can help you build a community of people who support, protect and nurture you.

Welcome to YOUR World

Look around. Like it or not, this is your world. No matter what it looks like, it's your canvas that you can paint any way you want. What kind of a painting you create is entirely up to you. So why not start painting it YOUR way? Why not live your life to the fullest? Even more important why not live it YOUR way, without self-judgment and without empowering the judgment of others to dictate your actions?

When you look around there is a very good chance that you may not feel like it is YOUR's yet. It may not be. But it can be. Just remember that life is a never ending journey. It changes constantly. So while you will never control everything you see with your eyes. You can direct how you interact with it. You can control how you respond to it. And in so doing, you can shape the world you live in.

It is a reasonable assumption that you are somewhere on your path toward personal evolution. It is also a reasonable assumption that you are working toward creating greater happiness. It is probably why you picked up this book. It is why you are still reading it. It is also why, after you have put it down you will hopefully continue to seek out your own truths and the truths of the world.

Just know that the path you are on does not have a start and a finish. It does not have a defined timeline. It is the path of evolution, and evolution is an ongoing process of eternal growth. Once you learned to breathe properly, you were able to meditate. Once you could meditate you could live a more mindful life and start to live with CaRE. Each of those practices evolved from the prior one and gave you the grounding you need to examine your layers and start to unpeel them; getting you closer and closer to your own simple truth. With each step you have gotten closer to evolving into the person you were meant to be.

Simple Truth

The only limits in life are those you set yourself.

You may ask what next? Does it all just stop when you become the person you want to be? The answer is no. There is eternal growth and evolution and expansion well beyond this life. It is why I call it an everlasting journey. Just by getting your life back in line with your Simple Truth, by living with compassion and in the present, you are already taking one of the biggest steps forward. So for now, just focus on getting back onto the proper path and on the here and now.

By now you have probably identified some issues you want to address, some habits you are better off without, and some hopes and dreams you would like to realize. These are the first steps to reaching your future. At the same time you have probably started to look back with a clearer vision of where you have come from. Your ability to look at your past and future will help you to live in the present and will continue to get clearer as you travel down your path.

Just remember that this is YOUR journey. It is YOUR path. It will not be the same path as anyone else. As you continue to experience and explore YOUR life, your path will continue to reward you with new experiences and new opportunities. It will give you an ever expanding view into all that your life can be. This is YOUR life. It is a journey without end. So enjoy it and embrace it. But also be vigilant. Be aware of yourself and the world around you. Acknowledge the truths as you learn them, and make good choices by living with CaRE. That will deliver the happiness you want, without having to seek it out.

Make Good Choices with CaRE

CaRE is more than just an acronym. It is a pause button to interrupt your internal programming that can be used at any time and in any situation. You just have to be grounded enough to use it. Whether you are making a life changing decision or responding to an impulse Living with CaRE enables you to stop what you are doing, take a moment to breathe and think about the consequences of your actions, so that you can make the right choices to keep your life moving in the direction you want it to move in.

Every day you are given opportunities to change your life. They do not come in the form of clouds parting and seas opening before you. They are not presented in the form of earth shattering events. Instead they are given to you in the little choices that you make every minute of every day. Every time you have a choice to make, you also have an opportunity to impact your life and evolve based on your knowledge of where you want to go. So don't wait for a profound decision to appear in order to change your life. Simply start making good choices every chance you get and your life will naturally flow in the right direction.

Like a snowball rolling down a hill, the small choices that you make quickly add up. They will land you at the right place at the right time, or at the end of a dark alley wondering how you ever got into your predicament. My tumors did not just pop up one day. They grew from the choices I made to work fourteen hours a day, seven days a week. They grew from my choice to entertain clients over a steak and a scotch instead of working out. They grew from my decision to try and build a company that was not what I wanted. They grew from my mind and body being so stressed and taxed that I was not able to handle the world I had created for myself and, had no energy left to keep my tumors at bay. Every time you have a choice to make you can act without thinking and by rote, or you can take thirty seconds to take three deep breaths and consider the consequences of your action, to choose the right path and make the right choice.

We all know you should not drive after drinking. Yet some people consistently put themselves in a no-win position at the end of a night of having to make a decision between paying for a taxi or breaking the law. But that decision would never have to be made if they had made good choices before arriving at their car door. Should they have a second cocktail knowing it would send them over the legal limit? Should they have even walked into the bar knowing they had to drive later? At any point they could have made a different choice that would have avoided the entire need to make a no-win decision.

It's the same for everyday life. Should you watch television or read a book when you come home exhausted? Should you buy another outfit knowing your credit card is maxed and you're going to have to write a rent or mortgage check at the end of the week? Should you continue seeing the person you're seeing if they make you feel less than your best? These are simple choices that have profound effects on your life. We all know what the right choices are. We just don't always make them when the opportunity arises. So next time, commit to taking a moment to think about the choices you have, so that you can make good choices.

To start making good choices, simply think about the word CaRE and the simple process those letters stand for. It is one of the single most important words you can say to yourself throughout your day. When you find yourself facing a choice, simply take three deep breaths and say the word "CaRE." It should remind you to stop or at least slow down; to take just a moment to ground yourself and think about what you are going to do so that you can start to make good choices.

This doesn't prevent you from having complete free will. You are still free to make the wrong decisions. You are free to ignore common sense. You are free to have that last goopy doughnut. But at least you are doing it because you want to, not because your old programming is telling you to. You will also find that you will start recognizing the choices you made when you find yourself feeling forced to face a no-win decision.

The process of making a good choice is part of the ongoing struggle we call life. Just because you use CaRE does not mean everything will instantly turn up roses. You will continue to make good choices and bad choices. You will continue to put yourself in awkward situations. But you will also start to take responsibility for the choices you make and for your life. You will start to recognize how you got to where you are and become aware of how simple choices can have tremendous effect on your life and your well being. Knowing that is a tremendous step to reprogramming yourself and your life.

There is no magic to it. There is only your desire to evolve YOUR life.

The next time you make a decision to do something, anything, stop for a moment and think to yourself:

> What **C**aused me to make this decision?
>
> How can I **R**espond to that Cause?
>
> What **E**ffect will my Response have on my future?
>
> Most important, how can I **a**ct so that my Response is the right one for ME?

It is YOUR life. So treat it like it is by taking ownership of the decisions you're making to make sure they are the right ones for YOU.

Live YOUR Happiness Now

If I told you that you could be happy right now if you gave up everything you owned, would you? If not, why not? Is it that your earthly possessions are more valuable than your happiness? This is something I cannot believe. Or is it that letting go of what is familiar to you is such a scary thought that you would risk a life of misery just for the sake of holding onto you're your car or home? This I can believe, because letting go of it is a very scary thought. It is going against everything that society has told you is right. It is going against the relentless pressures that corporate brands and their advertising are driving you toward.

But just remember, that is not your world.

Some people may tell you that in order to find happiness you must relinquish all of your earthly possessions. In a way, they are right. In many more ways they are over simplifying the world we live in today. One thousand, five hundred, even one hundred years ago, it was far easier to give up everything you owned because for many people, the conveniences we have today did not exist; and for many, being without some of those conveniences that were available did not make as large a difference.

Don't worry. I am not asking you to give up anything. I am simply asking you to rethink your relationship with the things you do have. To ask yourself why you have what you have, and why you desire the things that you desire. I am asking you to rethink the "why" behind the "what" that you own and to rethink the "why" behind the "what" that you do. Only after you start to do this can you reprogram your habits so that you can give up the things that are adding pain to your life, in order to focus on those things that will bring you happiness.

If I asked you to give up everything you owned I would then have to ask how you planned to shelter yourself from the cold and wind and rain. Who am I, or anyone, to say what kind of house you should or should not live in. Only you know when your home changes from a shelter to a burden. Some would say that you should give up your job if it is causing you stress. But then you would have to ask if the stress of having no money and knowing you would have no security in your old age is less than the stress you experience in your job?

> ***Simple Truth***
>
> *When you are present the world slows down to meet your pace.*

The answer to each of these questions is found in that sliding gray area called harmony. Paring down your life is essential to being happy. But how far you pare it down is entirely up to you. You and only you can answer that. Only you know where your balance and your harmony lay right now. Even more confusing, as you continue to peel back your layers and live your life in mindful awareness of the world around you, your perception of what you want will change.

As you grow and evolve, you will learn new things about yourself and the world around you. New technologies and conveniences will appear that will greatly change the world you live in. So the important task you will always wake up to is to ask yourself the surprisingly simple question, "What do you need versus what do you want?"

So ask yourself right now, "What do YOU want?" The real YOU does not want bigger houses or faster cars. The real YOU simply wants to be happy. The funny thing about the relationship between you and YOU is that you would be happy if you pursued what YOU wanted from the start. But that isn't how this world works. You were not born on day one, able to live in this world. You had to learn to survive first before you could evolve.

After you were born, you grew and learned how to live in the world. As you did so you created layers for yourself. These layers are a byproduct of learning how to live in the modern world. They prevented you from doing the one thing you wanted to do to be happy. Let's just say something got in the way. That something was called life. Well, now that you know how to live in the world, it's time to turn it all around and to return to the reason you're here at all, to live your happiness. Just as you need to return to your own Simple Truth in order to do this, you also need to return the physical world around you to the same point.

If at the end of the day you had a roof over your head and food on the table and you felt as if you were fulfilled and growing as a person, would you be happy? Most likely you would be. Unfortunately, like most people, you were told you needed more in order to be happy. So you imagined happiness as something you attain by owning a larger house or a driving a better car. You may have even thought that running away to an ashram or traveling the world to escape the realities would give you happiness. But what happens after your stay or your travels are over? What happens when you have to return to the world around you? You see, it's really the same thing. It's thinking that you can buy your way into happiness. When the real answer lies in simply being at peace with YOURSELF. And the only way you can get there is to remove everything that is not YOU and that is not true to your own Simple Truth.

If you're not ready to give up anything yet, ask yourself, what happens when you get that house of your dreams? What happens when you move in and find yourself walking through the empty rooms, staring at your possessions? How long does that happiness last? How long until you feel the need to invite others over to fill the emptiness. How long until you start renovating and upgrading? How long until you start to yearn for the next larger place, or a more remote location? It does not take long.

The sad thing is, many people turn to a stiff drink, toke or snort so that they do not have to face the one thing that would make them happy – themselves. Just look where most new-found celebrities find themselves after they have found success. Look what happens when that success is taken away. Does their entire world collapse?

> ***Simple Truth***
>
> *There is a difference between living in the past and remembering it so that you do not repeat it.*

More than likely it does. It happens to more people than you think. For many we even have a name for it. It's called a midlife crisis. But it really is the same thing. If your happiness depends on an event outside of yourself, sooner or later something will happen that you have no control over. Perhaps a fire, a flood, a burglar, or a divorce will come along and change your life. It will devastate you if your happiness depends on the objects around you rather than on yourself. Remember, you cannot control anything that is outside of you. You can only control how you respond to it.

So now that you know how many inches you have left in your tape measure, why not short-circuit your entire life experience by pursuing happiness from this point onward? If you have an impulse to buy something, take CaRE before you make a decision. Hit the "pause" button on your programming so that the choices you make are your own, and are in your own best interest for the long term.

One of the great regrets of my life is in not listening to my father when I went off to college. After asking me what I wanted to major in, he told me to take my time and explore different subjects. He told me to not worry so much about a defined major, but to use my time to try different things. He said I should take classes in art and even acting to see what I enjoyed. But I was in a very serious phase in my life, and decided that I had to pick a serious major. I listened to the wrong person and ended up with dual majors in accounting and business law. I also ended up with minors in mathematics and philosophy. Why? Because for whatever reason, I thought this person knew what was right for me.

It wasn't their fault and they weren't trying to be mean. They were simply giving me advice based on what they thought was best, not what was best for me.

In the end, I did well in those subjects. But I focused on the difficulties I was having and not on the successes I was having outside of class. I hosted dinner parties for my creative friends. I created a small business catering events for fraternities and sororities. I never thought about following my inner voice. Instead I just focused on my major and my life.

If I had taken the time to look at the things I was naturally good at and I had pursued them, who knows where my life would have ended up. In the end, my father was not very surprised when, after two years of work in the corporate world, I left for Los Angeles and the film industry.

Hind sight is twenty-twenty, but in looking back I would have made a horrible accountant and more than likely a so-so lawyer. I just never took the time to find out what it was I wanted to do. So instead of taking the time to figure it out, I plunged through life running faster and faster in the hopes that I would get somewhere. Where? I had no idea. Instead, if I had just admitted that I was never very interested in preparing detailed financial spread sheets nor in the art of suing someone I would have jump started my true life by a good ten years.

In today's media-rich world, it is difficult to separate yourself and your Simple Truth from the 24/7 message-cycle you are in. But having to be on call every minute of every day is not always worth the mansions owned. Which is why it is so important to identify what it is you want before you go after it – and no, rarely is it money.

Now that you are working to remove your old programs and your old layers, start to be vigilant about the "why" behind the "what" that you do so that you can evolve how you think and act on a daily basis so that your actions are truly in YOUR best interest. Do not let yourself fall into the easy path in response to the whims of the people and the world around you. Use CaRE. Only by being aware of the why behind whatever you do, can you begin to live the life YOU were meant to live. Only then can you find a balance between happiness and life in a society led by others.

So live your happiness, but do it with CaRE.

Enjoy Your Journey Warts & All

Life is about living. It really is that simple. It is about realizing and following the Simple Truth that you were born with. Not about a simple truth you think you should be living. So, use CaRE with care. Make sure the decisions you make are truly YOUR decisions. Remember that someone else's ideals may not necessarily be yours even though they can influence you greatly.

After all life is about enjoying your path of discovery while you are discovering it. Every step you take toward yourself can be a wonderful progression if you can embrace your perfections and your imperfections in the same way. Understanding this enables you to shape your life based on the realities of the world around you and the universe within you. Not on perceptions and expectations you have created for yourself.

If you can acknowledge and embrace both your strengths and your weaknesses equally, then you can grow in an honest and real manner. After all, your perfections and your imperfections are who you are. They are equally for who you will become. So learn to appreciate both in the same way. For only then can you be happy with the person you started out to be and the person you will grow into. Just do it slowly. If you try to rush your own evolution you risk throwing your physical world into turmoil and sliding backward instead of moving forward.

Strip away all that you comfortably can from your life. But also acknowledge that you have probably picked up some bad habits along the way. So take baby steps toward your own Simple Truth. It's not a race because there really is no finish line. There is simply a rejoining with the person you were meant to be.

Be diligent and aware so that you are moving forward, but also remember you need to be comfortable with yourself. Also remember that you have this life to live. So do so with every ounce of energy you have.

If you can reduce your lifestyle so that you need less money, then you gain the freedom to work in a job that you enjoy more, even if it pays less. If you pay less attention to the call of advertising, then you reduce your need to keep up with the Joneses, and you can spend more time living your own Simple Truth. Remember that your journey is more important than your destination. If you simply live your life by your own Simple Truth every day, happiness will be the wonderful byproduct of it.

This is why it is important to acknowledge that the world will change around you. The only constant is YOU. So follow YOUR Truth without clinging to past fears or future expectations. To do so is to invite pain into your life. To hate yourself for what you think are weaknesses will only sink yourself into despair. So embrace who you are, warts and all. For that is the way to happiness.

Your Simple Truth Is Your Compass

As you evolve and the world changes around you, your Simple Truth will the only constant. It is your Life's Compass that will enable you to stay on your path no matter what life presents to you. It will give you the grounding you need to interrupt your programming with CaRE so that you have control over the choices you make and the path you walk on. The knowledge of your Simple Truth will enable you to balance your actions with CaRE, no matter where you find yourself. It will help you to stay within sight of your path, even if you fall off of it.

> ***Simple Truth***
>
> *You only need one small act every day to change your life.*

No matter what you do, the opportunity for new experiences will always present themselves. Some of these will be welcome, others – not so much. It is up to you to decide what you want to experience and explore. As long as you make your choices with full awareness of the consequences of your actions you will continue to grow.

Just keep in mind that the well lived life is a life of moderation. Moderation does not mean living a life of denial or abstinence. It means striking a balance in everything that you do so that you can enjoy some of the pleasures that the world has to offer, but so that you also remain grounded enough to never lose yourself in them.

Take the Time to Appreciate Beauty & Art

Living with CaRE is not just about avoiding the pitfalls of life. It is also about making a conscious decision to enjoy all that life has to offer in an aware state of living. If there is one gift we all share, it is the ability to appreciate beauty. We are endowed with the ability to appreciate a beautiful poem or work of art. We can grow after experiencing an object of beauty. We can fall in love with an image that moves us. To throw that gift away, to ignore our own abilities is to miss a very valuable piece of what it is to be human.

Look around you. You will find natural beauty, manmade beauty, intellectual beauty, sexy ugly beauty. There are so many types of beauty we have run out of ways to classify it. So rather than look at the world through a narrow field of vision based on someone else's definition of beauty, take the time to find the beauty in everything. It's far too easy to dismiss something as ugly, or "less than," just because the media tells you so. It's far more intriguing to search for the beauty before you, and far more rewarding.

So don't let society rob you of the pleasure of finding beauty no matter where you go. Don't empower someone else by letting them direct you on what to buy or what color to paint a room. Allow yourself to appreciate the beauty in yourself, in others, in the hidden delights that you find along your way, and especially in the work that someone else has created. It can be as simple as an etching on a rock. It can be as detailed as the stitching of a leather craftsperson. It can be as complicated as a circuit board. We all find beauty in different things. We all have different tastes and passions and desires. What is emotionally powerful to one person, may not be as powerful to someone else. Remember to enjoy your own view of beauty and to appreciate the view someone else holds.

Beauty and art are extremely subjective concepts. Like your own journey in life, choose to take the time and enjoy the beauty of the world around you. Choose to explore the idea behind what the artist or craftsperson was doing when they created the music, the meal, the shirt, the handbag or the painting before you. Use CaRE to enjoy the journey they were taking, as well as the final form. Enjoy the fact that someone else can appreciate beauty, even if it is not your idea of beauty.

Laugh at Your Mistakes and Evolve

Everything in our universe moves in a circle. Ocean waves, weather patterns, the orbits of the planets, even life itself moves in a circular motion. It curls back on itself, it spins and turns, it is very much a part of a larger circle. Your successes and your mistakes come back to you. But whether you grow from them or not depends on how you relate to them.

Know that there will always be chances to do more. Be comforted by the fact that there will always be opportunities ahead of you. Most important learn to laugh at the events in your life, no matter how dire and how serious they seem. If you allow yourself to get caught up in the fact that you did something wrong, then you will fail to see the opportunity that arises from it.

Along your path, you will slip and fall. It's a very real part of evolution. Just don't dwell on your slips, your trips and your falls. Instead, use them as a lesson. Think about getting up, think about how far you got before you tripped. Think about the lessons you learned along the way. Falling down is very different than failure. One is a lesson you take with you; the other is never seeing what you were supposed to learn. If you see yourself starting to stumble, use CaRE to start making small choices to pick yourself up.

Some people worry so much about failing they doom themselves before they have a chance to succeed. If you see nothing but risk, then you will succumb to it. If you keep looking for opportunities, you may slip, you may even fall, but you will never fail. So, relax. Enjoy the ride and don't worry about the inevitable.

You are going to slip. You're going to say something stupid at a party. You're going to misquote a number. You are going to make a mistake. How do I know this? Because I have done it more times than I care to remember. I also know I will do it again. But I will not let the specter of failure prevent me from growing and evolving; from trying something new.

Thomas Edison made thousands of mistakes before creating a light bulb that worked. He held over 1,083 patents, and only a rare few actually made it to the real world. When Mr. Edison failed with a light bulb; he looked at it as an experiment. He noted what he had done wrong, readjusted his plans, and he kept improving on his design until it worked.

Every spiritual leader we have had made their share of mistakes and had their moments of doubt along the way before finding their own way. This is exactly what you need to do in life. When faced with what you think is an insurmountable obstruction or a no-escape failure, you need to stop and view it as an experiment, as an adventure, and move on. As difficult as it is to detach yourself, you need to take a step backward and observe your situation from a distance. You need to rid yourself of the emotions and influences that prevent you from making an intelligent, unbiased decision so that you can make the right one. Most important you need to stop looking for someone or something to blame. If you are to live YOUR life, you need to take responsibility for the decisions you made and live with the results – for better or worse.

Simple Truth

Amid the excitement, mind your words. They will live long into the future and have a lasting effect.

This is why I laugh at my mistakes. It doesn't relieve me of any responsibility, but it does enable me to break the cycle, to learn from my mistakes and move on.

Before I got married, I remember waking up to the disastrous end of a short-lived relationship. The person I had gotten serious about had called me on the phone to say it was not working. It was the old fashioned version of a modern day, text message break up. Needless to say, I was miserable. After a few days of moping around I looked at myself in the proverbial mirror and said, "I am sick of waking up alone. I love the life that I have, but I want to share it. I want someone I can sit on a porch with at the age of eighty and laugh about all our memories together."

I remember actually laughing at myself for admitting to such a feeling and for admitting the need for love and companionship. But I realized it was true. I also realized my current approach to dating was not working very well. So, instead of running out and looking for a new girlfriend, I stopped and asked myself what I wanted. I actually started a list of past girlfriends and wrote down the things I liked and did not like about each of them. As I did, I started seeing some of the same things in the personalities of the relationships that worked, and that did not work. What amazed me was how simple the list turned out to be, and how consistent the patterns were.

I found that I wanted someone from a particular part of the United States not because I liked a particular part of the country, but because I enjoyed the sensibilities that seem to come from people raised there. I loved someone with a sense of independence and a can-do attitude. I began to realize what I liked and didn't like in my life.

Then I took the time to use my relationship failures to create a mental list that I kept as a reminder of what I really wanted. It was hardly scientific, but it prevented me from making the same mistakes I had made in the past. It kept me on track to walking away from some relationships that weren't heading anywhere until I found someone I could spend my life with, and not just another date.

I am not saying that you need to replace passion with a list, because passion should be a part of that list. I am saying that no matter what the subject, you can learn from your mistakes. You can find love, happiness and success by applying what you have learned from your mistakes to make better decisions in the future.

From love to light bulbs you are able to turn failures into opportunities by using the lesson you learn with CaRE. But to do that you have to be aware of who YOU are, what YOU want, and why. You have to be able to step back and look at yourself and your actions in an unbiased way so that you can improve your life. If you can separate yourself from the events and apply what you have learned to your future actions, then anything is possible. As Einstein once said, "the definition of insanity is doing the same thing over and over again, and hoping for a different result."

So the next time something goes wrong, take a breath. Take a step back. Laugh if you must, but look at what just occurred from a new perspective. Walk yourself through CaRE, and think of how to evolve your thinking for the future. The key to turning a mistake into a life lesson is to not dwell on it. To not let it have power over your life. Instead, acknowledge it and learn from it. Then move on with an understanding of how not to repeat it.

You are not alone when you do this. We all learn more by living through our own mistakes and by observing the mistakes made by others. I imagine this is why you are reading this book. You want to learn from someone who has made mistakes – me – so that you can stop yourself from repeating them.

Exercise – What Does YOUR CaRE Look Like?

We all make choices in our lives, some large and some small. Some have an immediate impact, and some you may not even think mattered. Even if you found out later they did.

Take a few deep breaths and close your eyes. Now take a moment to visualize a recent choice you made. Pick something small and with less significance in your life to begin with. Walk through the event and visualize what you were doing when the

Cause happened. Visualize what you were thinking, or not thinking about. Be honest, were you on auto-pilot?

Now, walk through the CaRE process and just think how you could have made a different choice. Find the one point in time when you could have interrupted your process. Think about how you could have stopped yourself from jumping to respond before you thought out your answer.

What would have happened if you had given a different answer? If it was a business situation and you took an extra fifteen seconds, would it have ended the deal? Or changed it in your favor? If it was a fight with someone you cared about, what could you have done to sidestep the emotional argument and focused on the facts at hand?

Now project that same situation into the future. Think about how you would handle it differently. It may seem silly, but in doing this exercise, you can start to train yourself to think before you act. You can train your instinct to think before responding; which is essential if you want to run your life the way you want it to be run.

Harmonize Your Life With Mindfulness

Being mindful requires doing more than just being aware of yourself and the world around you. It means recognizing issues as they arise so that you can attend to them before they become problems. It means responding once you start to truly see the people and the world around you as they truly are so that you can avoid the pitfalls of life and move yourself in a positive direction. If you fail to take action once you become conscious of, and embrace the inevitability of change, then why be conscious at all?

If you know that the world around you will change, if you know that the people around you will change, then you will be more prepared for that change when it occurs. That means you can spend less time and energy worrying about the fact that things do change, and more time adapting to it. To evolve with the changing world you do not need to know exactly what will change you simply need to be aware of the world's temporal nature, so that you can accept the changes and evolve with them.

By living a mindful life you will be in a better position to embrace the world around you and grow in harmony with it no matter what happens.

Love Your Social Net

By nature humans are social creatures. We naturally want to be with others. It's in our genes. It is also one of the most important evolutionary advantages we have over all other animals. Our ability to work and band together in tight knit groups enabled us to overcome every obstacle that has come our way, at least thus far.

In simpler terms, people simply like people. We have all, at times wanted to be alone. But in the end we seek others because we simply like having people around us. There is nothing wrong with this or weak about this. Why should there be? Having friends and family you can rely on is not only fun, but it has far-reaching benefits for your health, well-being, and yes, survival. There are more than enough studies that show how just having supportive people around you positively affects your life. There are also studies that show how just talking through problems can reduce the stress they cause. This means that you can never have too many positive relationships in your life.

This is why it's so strange that the concept of networking has such a dirty connotation to it. It instantly conjures images of some conniving individuals climbing the social ladder, stabbing people in the back on their way to the top. When that is not what a real social network is really about.

A real social network is a group of friends and family who share with each other, who help each other and who look out for each other because they want to. It is a group of friends who know they can ask for help when they need it. And believe me, at one point or another in your life, you will need help.

Someone once said, "The difference between being homeless and having a home is the network of friends someone has."

They're not all that wrong. If you have a safety net of people that you can rely on then you will always have solid ground to stand on. Without a safety net you go through life without a buffer. When something happens the impact is immediate and there is nowhere to turn. Yet with one, you have a bit of protection against the whims of the world.

Even if you cherish your quiet time, step out and start to cultivate your network of friends and build your own safety net. Believe it or not, every once in a while you will need help from someone. You may even need help from a lot of people. So the more you do to create and nurture your safety net the better.

> ***Simple Truth***
>
> *When you say yes to someone, make sure you're not saying no to yourself.*

No, this doesn't mean you have to be a social butterfly. It certainly does not mean you have to entertain people you don't like. It simply means that with a little bit of effort you can create relationships, on any number of levels, to build and mend your net.

All you have to do is just allow yourself to enjoy the people in your life. Talk with them and laugh with them. Be aware and mindful of those around you and appreciate all that they have to offer. Learn to appreciate all that you have to give to them. Give yourself the time to reach out to them. There doesn't need to be any strategy behind this, and certainly no manipulation. Simply allow yourself to enjoy being around the people that you like.

Think of it as creating your own tribe of people who support your goals, dreams and Simple Truths. In return, just take the time to support their goals, dreams and Simple Truths, even if you might question them. All of a sudden the idea of a safety net shouldn't sound so daunting. All you have to d is be mindful of those around you and reach out to the individuals who are aligned with your direction. If you can do that your net will create itself.

Stay in touch regularly through a quick email, a note or with a Facebook account. The fact that fewer people write letters is exactly why you should start. It makes a lasting impression that goes a long way in building and maintaining your social net.

Just be careful that you do not overextend yourself. Remember life is about balance and harmony. So set aside time to recharge your batteries. Understand when to say "yes" and when to say "thank you, but not right now".

Building friendships does not mean you have to accept every invitation that comes your way. Nor should you always refuse events simply because staying home is easier. Be judicious of who you follow up with, but also trust your friends as a way to meet new people. You never know where it might lead.

If you're really stuck in a rut, take a step out and start doing the things that you have always wanted to do. Pick a charity you are passionate about and volunteer. Visit a museum or try a cooking class even if you already know how to. Simply do whatever it is you enjoy most.

People gravitate toward others who enjoy the things they enjoy. People seek out those who understand and agree with them. Even if you don't meet anyone new, the worst thing that can happen is that you end up doing the things you enjoy doing anyway.

Just be mindful of the net you are weaving. While you need to create a supportive network, you also need to be careful that it remains true to your Simple Truth. While you need to be accepting, understanding, open-minded and compassionate with everyone around you, you also need to be careful and protective of YOUR time and YOUR world. After all, creating a net that reaches too far can quickly collapse under its own weight, which is not the positive direction you want to move your life.

Be aware of your own habits that wander toward co-dependency and collecting friends. There are a lot of people with unhealthy habits who latch on to someone who supports their habits. As you grow and start to remove unhealthy relationships, be careful not to replace them with people who bring the same unhealthy habits back into your life.

> ***Simple Truth***
>
> *My truth is not your truth. We must each find out own and seek out their intersections in order to be happy.*

This can apply to family and long-term friends, and can include some bonds that are difficult to break. But in order to grow, you have to replace the bad with the new, even if for a short time. You can always step back from a relationship so that you can redefine it.

So if someone keeps pressuring you to conform to their dress code, their beliefs, or their way of living, simply step away until you are ready to re-engage them at your own level. That is the best way to create a healthy set of friends that truly support your growth.

There is No Work/Life Balance – Only Life

I don't know how else to say it than this: YOU were not put here to work. YOU were put her to live. Which is why there is no such thing as a work/life balance; there is only life.

Work is a component of your life. It should never over-ride your life, and certainly shouldn't be in competition with your life. It should not be the sole reason you are alive. Your work should support the life that you want to live, not undermine it.

Using the words "work/life balance" is something many people do to soften the truth about their lives. Instead of saying "I'm unhappy with my life," they say "I have to find my work/life balance." Rarely are their problems in life just related to their job alone. It's as if finding a way to spend less time at a job will solve everything when it won't.

Have you ever heard someone who loves their job complain about their work/life balance? They don't because they love what they do. For them, life is in balance. Have you ever heard someone in a bad relationship complain about their relationship/life balance? They don't. Instead they complain about a bad marriage or a bad relationship.

For whatever reason, we have elevated our work to the level of our lives. Yet your job, your relationship, your marriage, the time you spend at the gym, these are just different activities within your life.

Instead of trying to find balance between each of them recognize that you cannot do everything. So think about which part of your life is most important to you and which gives you more than they require from you. Ask yourself if each component of your life actually supports you or undermines you, so that your life becomes the priority for everything you do.

Yes, this is different for everyone. If you spend too much time on your relationship, your work, or even your time at the gym, it can create an imbalance and chip away at your life as a whole. We have all seen someone at the gym who is in fantastic shape, yet seems like a very lonely person. We also all know someone who loves what they do and spends more time at work than might seem normal, but is as happy as can be.

If you love your relationship then take that happiness into your work and let it affect how you manage the people around you. If you love your time at the gym, then take the adrenaline and endorphins that you release there into the other parts of your life to energize them. If you love your work, then don't be afraid to talk about it. Embrace the happiness you gain from it.

Instead of seeking a balance between your professional and personal lives, think about bringing them together so that all of the components of your life are in harmony. If you feel trapped in a horrible job then strive to find a new one, even if it means changing your personal lifestyle so that you wouldn't need the higher salary. If you are trapped in a relationship with someone who doesn't understand or support your dreams, then it may be time to find someone who does. In the end, your life will suffer for the disharmony one segment of your life can bring, no matter what side it comes from.

Just realize that your happiness does not require that you split your life into equal segments. Everyone is different. Some people thrive on rising early and dedicating their morning to work. Others prefer to sleep until noon and start their day after the sun has crested. Some people love working with numbers and solving engineering problems. Others exist for the personal contact they have in working with people. Others still find the joy they seek in tending a home and raising children.

None of these people wants to do what the others do. None wants the other's schedule. But each can find extreme pleasure and value in what they enjoy doing.

While not everyone is seeking the same balance in their lives, everyone is seeking to find harmony across everything they do. So be mindful of what those around you enjoy. Learn how their harmony comes together. Learn to support them in their goals, even if you don't understand them.

Being mindful is not just about seeing the world from your own perspective, but seeing it from an unbiased perspective, so that you can enjoy someone else's success, even if you may not agree with their perspective, or where they happen to have found their balance.

Realize that there is no magical work/life ratio that has led to happiness. It all depends on who a specific person is, and what their own Simple Truths are. So before you worry about finding your own balance, find out what your Simple Truths are and follow them. Let that guide you into a profession you enjoy that balances your lifestyle with your life.

The Same But Different

Every one of you is unique. You can see it just by opening your eyes. You see it in the faces and physiques of the people around you. You see it in the way different people act and react. Yet with all of the differences you notice in others, we are also almost identical.

With all the variations that you can see, did you know that our genes differ by just 0.5%? That means 99.5% of who you are is identical to everyone around you. As if that weren't enough, the genes of chimpanzees and humans vary by just 2%. 80% of a cow's genes are similar to those of a human. So while we are all different, we are all infinitely more similar than we are different, not just with other humans, but with the rest of the animals who inhabit the earth. Even though you must celebrate what makes you unique, you must also celebrate the things that you share with everyone else.

Learn to enjoy your own show without being self-conscious. Learn to appreciate what others can do without being jealous. Appreciate the 99.5% that we all share.

Be mindful of your strengths and weaknesses as well as those of the people around you. Be aware of what you are capable of and what limitations you may have by being mindful of your own abilities. You can set your sights accordingly and live in harmony with the physicality of your world. With hard work you can always push your natural born abilities to their limits and beyond. History is full of men and women who have done incredible things when they set their will to it, and the power of the mind and spirit are far from being understood.

> ***Simple Truth***
>
> *Birds of a feather flock together.*

Just don't let your happiness depend on how you compare with others. Let it depend on how similar you are. That 0.5% difference is often the difference between war and peace. If you must compete, then do so with yourself. Strive to constantly improve what you do so that you grow in all things, and not at the cost of someone else.

Stop Swatting At Flies

When I was very young and caught up in the world of two older brothers, very frequently one or all three of us would get caught up in some big fight over who had what or who did what. My mother would break it up and she would always ask us the same question "what were you fighting about?" We would all shrug.

We would all shrug and separate, until whatever it was we were fighting about was forgotten and we created some new game for us to play.

We were not fighting over anything important. We were like a pack of dogs in a dog park chasing each other over a stick. The stick was not what was important. The fact that another dog had the stick was.

The same was true for my brothers and me. We weren't fighting because we didn't like each other. We were fighting because that was what we were programmed to do. Somebody did X and somebody else did Y and it just escalated until it was just another tussle.

I see this in married couples all the time. One person does something that annoys their partner, who responds with a little nudge of their own. Each keeps elevating the stress levels, step by step, until before you know it an argument has started that has nothing to do with anything, other than one person trying to stay ahead of the other person's comments.

It's what I call swatting at flies. We lose the real reason we are doing something and get sidetracked by our base programming, as if we are on automatic pilot. We try to swat flies rather than fix the hole in the screen door.

"Why don't you just walk away?" My mother would ask while separating us. We would all just shrug. It was our answer for everything. Because there really was no reason we were fighting, other than needing to get the last word in, to being the last one to hold the stick.

You might notice this in most arguments. At some point a discussion quickly changes from trying to be right, to trying to be on top, from resolving an issue, to responding to basic human nature and programming.

It took me years to realize that all my life I had been doing exactly what the pack of dogs does with a stick. I wasn't chasing after the stick, I was chasing after the dog that had the stick. I didn't want the stick. I wanted what the stick represented. The funny thing is everyone else was doing the same thing.

Be mindful when you stop fixing the hole in the screen and start swatting at the flies getting in. Be aware when you stop pursuing your goal and start pursuing what someone else has. Be aware when you stop discussing and start arguing just to get the last word in. If you do that, you will never mend the broken screen, you will just spend the rest of your days swatting at flies.

Simple Truth

The less reactive you are, the stronger you become.

In life, the person with the larger salary, the better office, the nicer car, the seemingly more perfect family is just a distraction. They are the flies you keep swatting after. What they represent keeps you from pursuing your own happiness. They will keep you chasing after different goals. Meanwhile, the one reality you have, your life, will pass you by.

One way of pursuing your Simple Truth is to try to remove the distractions that keep you from living your own life. But no matter how many distractions you remove, more will always appear. If instead, you live mindfully, you will be able to see the distractions as unimportant to your life, and will be able to ignore them so that you can patch the real problem.

How you respond to the world around you is always up to you. You can either decide to respond to a distraction or to simply walk away. You see, living mindfully is not so much about focusing on what is there, as it is being aware of what is not there so that you can stay present and focused to pursue your own Simple Truth no matter what life throws at you.

That will empower you to stop living on automatic pilot, jumping from one distraction to the next, and enable you to focus on the larger issues that truly matter.

Being mindful will enable you to use CaRE as you make choices in your life. It will help you remove the outside influences, the old attachments, and the superficial objects that you have clung to until now. These are the things that cause you pain, because they keep you running in a circle, rather than after your dreams, your goals, and your Simple Truths.

If there is a hole in a screen that is letting in flies, swatting at each and every fly will solve nothing. You will simply continue to swat flies for the rest of your life. Instead, ignore the flies and mend the hole. Only then will you stop the flies from getting in.

Possess Nothing You Can't Afford To Lose

No matter where you find yourself, remember that you have no control over the world around you. You can only control how you respond to events that transpire. That does not mean you are powerless to pursue your life, or that the only response you can have to the events of the world is to shrug your shoulders and walk away.

It means that the less baggage you have with you, the more nimble you will be when something does happen. The fewer fears, biases and attachments that you have, the more you are free to live mindfully and to guide your life in the direction you want to go.

Look around you and ask yourself, if you lost something that you cherished how much pain would it cause? Would you feel loss, regret, or anger? Perhaps all of them depending on how attached you were to a given object.

How much pain would it cause if you lost some of your favorite things? Would losing a cherished heirloom cause you the same level of pain as if you lost your most expensive handbag? It might, but it would also be a different kind of pain.

It's important to recognize this. Because it is not the object that is valuable, but the memories and emotions that it carries with it. It is the value that you or someone else has created for the object that makes it valuable.

After their parents passed away a family I know kept their childhood home even though none of the brothers or sisters in the family lived near it. In the first year, it was a sentimental place for them to go on family holidays. In the second year the costs of maintaining the house started to add up. Each one of them had to cancel some of the things their own families did in order to hold onto that house. In the third year, after much wrangling they decided to finally put it on the market. It sold quickly and without much fuss.

They were pained by the loss of the house and missed having it in their lives. But I remember hearing from them after their first Thanksgiving without the old house. They had pooled the money they no longer had to spend to keep up the old family home, and used it to rent a house in the country for a week-long family vacation. They were amazed at how wonderfully the week went. They all felt freer and lighter, able to talk about the future and not just the past. They spent their time sharing the same family stories they had told for years. But they also talked about where they would go for the next year's Thanksgiving. For the rest of the year they planned the next location for their next family vacation.

They realized their childhood house had become as much a trap as it was a home. In the end it was not the home that brought their family together, but each other. Without the monolith of their old home to hold them back they moved on.

The same can be true for a handbag, a watch, or a family heirloom. It is not the physical object that is valuable, but the energy you give to it. If that energy comes from memories and heartfelt emotions, it can be a very powerful thing. If that energy was created through an expensive advertising campaign, it can end up sucking up your own energy; convincing you to want and need something that really isn't that important to you.

The energy an object carries with it is what evokes the feelings and memories that are important, not the physical properties of whatever it is you own. In some cases the fear of losing something becomes so powerful it can prevent you from enjoying your life.

So if you cannot afford to lose something, consider whether you own it or it owns you, because in the end, it may just end up owning you.

Take the time to look at the objects around you. Be aware of how you feel when you see a particular item. Start a list of some of what you own if you must, and ask yourself, is this something I really need? Is it essential to living my life? If not, label it expendable.

That doesn't mean you have to throw it away. It just means that you need to remember it is not an essential part of your life. It might be nice to have, but it may also add stress to your life, or it may even create unhappiness. If so, consider letting it go.

In the same way you can look at an object and ask if it makes you happy. You can also ask <u>why</u> it makes you happy. Or <u>why</u> it does not. How happy or sad something makes you is often not as important as the "why" behind your emotion.

If you have a pair of shoes that you love, the fact that they make you feel good about yourself every time you wear them is a bonus on top of the fact that they protect your feet. However, if your own self-worth is tied to wearing those shoes, if you feel less than yourself if you're not wearing them then they may have started to own you. You have lost a piece of your self confidence, your own self-worth to those shoes. As absurd as it sounds, in today's society it happens all the time.

Even if you haven't paid for something, it if is an heirloom or a gift, it can have the same power over you. If something reminds you of a misery in your life, why hold onto it? Why remind yourself of a time or a person that undermined your happiness and self worth? Even if something brings you happiness, it can still hold you back by not allowing you to move past an event in your life, rather than enabling you to seek other adventures, experiences and even the life you now want to live.

It is up to you, and only you, to decide whether an item is an emotional attachment for you. Nobody else knows what is in your heart. You have to be strong, but you also have to be honest with YOURSELF. Only then can you be free to live your life YOUR way.

Daily Mindful Living

Living mindfully is simply a way to extend your meditation outside of a sitting formal practice. It enables you to live in a state of heightened awareness so that you can be in greater control of your thoughts, your emotions and your happiness.

Living mindfully will not remove the ups and downs of your life. It will however change how your everyday experiences influence you. It will change your relationship to the world around you and the life you are living.

To live mindfully is not the same as living in a perfect world. The clouds will not part and give you sunshine every day. People will not instantly be friendlier. But you will be able to appreciate life's events, regardless of whether they are positive or negative. You will be able to consciously decide whether you will empower an outside event and enable it to affect your life, or slide by with barely a ripple.

Losing a job, getting a divorce, struggling to separate unruly children, these are the everyday events that can make life a struggle if you let them. Even making the effort to understand someone you love requires work. They are not happy events or sad events. They are simply events that you choose to make good or bad, happy or sad. Regardless of how you allow them to affect your life, they can all be appreciated as experiences and as lessons in your life.

It is up to you to decide how involved you will become in the events of your life. You can either let them overpower your days and nights, or you can separate yourself from them and witness them as a dispassionate observer.

You may say to yourself, "but I have to be involved in this." No you don't. Every event in your life can be observed if you separate yourself from the actions going go on around you. If you watch them from a slightly remote place, then you will enable yourself to appreciate the challenges and elations that life inevitably brings you, but from a position from which you can manage them, rather than a place where the event manages you.

All that you need to do to live mindfully on a daily basis is to practice mindful living every day. It may sound ridiculous, but it's true. Just start small, start by simply being aware of where you are and what you are feeling. If you continue to do this, your mind will do the rest.

You will start to find that you naturally become more mindful of what is going on around you. You will simply stop trying to anticipate what others are doing or why they are doing what they do. You will stop trying to guess as to the why behind the what that others are doing. You will just accept that they are who they are, that they act the way they act because it is who they are. You will find that you will just live in the moment, aware of the world around you.

Simple Truth

Don't let a temporary emotion make a permanent decision in your life.

You may find that you will start to view the tirades of your boss or the nit-picking of a family-member differently. You will probably start to see them as ridiculous, even laughable, rather than a source of stress. You will witness a paradigm shift in the world because you no longer allow yourself to get caught up in the actions of the world. You will find that the actions that used to affect so much of your life will fade away like mist with little effect on your life.

As you go through your day in a mindful state, you will find yourself constantly waking up to new truths about yourself and the world around you. Some of these will come as sudden flashes of awareness that are so powerful you cannot but help to see behind the very fabric of your reality. Others may creep in more subtly as if someone has slowly pulled back a curtain that has kept the light from shining on you. Either way you will become aware just how much of your life has been spent responding to the world around you rather than living your life.

There is no magic to it. There is only a greater awareness of the world and a heightened understanding of your relationship to it. For many of you, it will be the first time that you are truly in control of your life. Enjoy that feeling; treat it and those around you with respect and compassion. Don't judge those around you no matter what they do. Simply understand how your life used to be and how it can be now that it is truly YOUR life.

Minding Pain

Living mindfully is not just about managing your responses to the larger issues of the world. It is a very powerful practice to rethink the way you interact in all parts of your life.

Several weeks ago I was walking down the street. A child of perhaps six was running to his mother in a park near where I live. He tripped as children do and fell down. Instantly his face contorted into a mask of everything you never want a child to experience – pain, fear, terror. He was on the verge of crying when his mother reached down and touched his head.

She said, "It's okay. It doesn't hurt. You're just a little frightened. That's all." He looked up at her and she kept talking in her soothing tone. "You just didn't expect that did you? It's okay, you're not hurt, you're just a little shaken."

He looked at his hands and saw that there was no blood. He looked at his knees and saw everything was okay. In seconds he was up and running off to some other children in the playground. She noticed me looking and gave me a quick smile and shrugged.

It was an incredible lesson in how we are programmed to respond to unexpected events and to pain. Our instant reaction to an unexpected event like falling down is one of sheer terror. Our natural response is not based on pain, but on the expectation of pain and a very complex array of emotions and feelings. We forget that pain is not just a simple physical sensation, but a combination of shock, fear, hate, loathing even shame, that come in a paralyzing wave.

When you get hurt, physically or emotionally, you instantly recoil from whatever caused the pain. It is your body's way of protecting you. As you get hurt, you may freeze up and go into a bit of shock as your brain tries to register what just happened. Then your emotions come into play, which generates an adrenaline spike. It is a normal mechanism as your body prepares for a fight or flight response, or until it can figure out exactly what just happened. The result is that your mind and body go through a rapid fire series of responses as you register the pain and catalogue it so that you do not repeat your mistake again.

In seconds, your mind and body may create an overwhelming feeling of hate for whatever it is that caused pain. You may want to strike out at it. Some people actually do. They throw pots when they burn their hands while cooking.

You might feel loathing that you recoiled rather than confronted whatever it is that caused the pain. You may also feel shame in how you reacted. So instead of just dealing with the pain of tripping, or touching a hot stove, or getting dumped by someone you were seeing, you are now dealing with a half dozen emotions that make the pain seem bigger than it ever was.

There are two things to remember when dealing with pain. First, pain is inevitable – both physically and emotionally. It will occur at some level throughout your entire life. It is one way that we all learn and grow. Touch a hot skillet once and you will remember to test it before grabbing it the next time. Meet a person who stabs you in the back, and you avoid that type of person in the future.

Next, pain is just as much about the past as it is about the present. A painful event will cause your brain to quickly try to categorize it by relating it to past experiences. When you are going through a break-up, it is not just this breakup that is painful. It is the memory of all your past relationships that comes into play. That brings up years of feelings of failure, shame and frustration that you have to deal with, including your recent spat. Not all of these are relevant to your present situation, but there they are.

Applying mindfulness to your pain can help you separate the immediate physical or emotional discomfort from the memory of past pain. When I recovered from my most recent surgery I shocked the doctors by the speed of my recovery. They couldn't find a reason to keep me in the hospital for more than a few days. I credit much of this to weaning myself off of the painkillers quickly so that my mind was clear and able to focus on healing rather than blurred by medication. There is no medical evidence that meditating as often as I did after my surgeries helped me. But it enabled me to focus on healing, not on the trauma I just went through. When you are caught up in the trauma of an event it saps energy that could have otherwise enabled you to heal and move on with your life.

The next time you experience pain, apply the concept of CaRE to your experience. After your body reacts, stop and take a few breaths. Bring your attention to the pain that you are feeling and identify what actually hurts. Separate the physical pain from the emotional. Separate past experiences from your present situation. Most important realize that the physical and emotional pain you are feeling do not need to rule the rest of your life.

If you are aware there are feelings that you have attached to your pain, you can diminish the power they have over you. So next time, ask yourself if any of these feelings are part of your experience. If so, you can get past the perceived "pain" and focus on the real pain in order to get on with the rest of your life.

Ask yourself if you are feeling any of these emotions:

Anger – hatred for whatever caused your pain

Shame – thinking that you should have acted differently or more stoically

Frustration – asking yourself "why me?" or thinking that bad things only happen to you when pain happens to everyone

Guilt – feeling that you should have done things differently and are more responsible for what went wrong, regardless of what actually happened

Projecting – thinking ahead to all of the potential outcomes from a simple instance

Fright – afraid that whatever happened will keep happening for the rest of your life

The next time you experience pain, physically or emotionally, think of the child in the playground. Think of how quickly he learned that the shock of a fall hurts a lot more than the fall itself, or the physical harm it did to his body. Then think about how quickly he got back into life and started laughing again.

You can do the same thing with three deep breaths, a bit of mindful awareness and a touch of CaRE.

Minding Fear

It's been said that fear is the mind-killer. In a way it is. Fear can have a numbing and paralyzing effect on anyone when they give into it. It is yet another emotion linked to survival that can quickly overpower all the logic you can muster and rule your life.

If left alone fear can turn into paralyzing phobias that no logic in the world can get rid of. Learn to overcome the fears in your life and a new world will open up to you.

Like pain, fear is a complex combination of emotions that is as much about the past as it is about the present. Fear is your body's way of preventing you from getting hurt. Your mind works at lightning speed when it finds itself in any kind of situation – especially one with unknown consequences. It applies past experiences to your current situation to keep you safe. If your current situation is similar to a past experience that ended badly, the resulting emotion you are given is fear – getting you ready for a fight or flight response.

It is why you are afraid when you get to the edge of a plane, preparing to jump at fifteen thousand feet even though you have a parachute on. It is why you think twice about entering a dark alley when nobody else is around. It is also why we say that "change is scary." All of this is based on your brain telling you that you are in an unsafe situation. Centuries ago, change meant a real potential to get hurt. Yet in today's world, change is part of living, and change keeps happening faster and faster.

In most instances your innate fear is a good thing. After all, it has kept people alive for forty thousand years. But it was also something that our ancestors learned to overcome in order to advance. Our ancestors grew and evolved because they overcame the fear of change and moved to new locations, they overcame their fear of the unknown and tried new foods, they experimented with new cures, and they risked change.

In today's world rarely do the risks you take have immediate life or death impact. Instead, moving to a new city to start over may set you back a year, but rarely will it kill you. Taking six months off from a job to travel the world may delay your career, but I have yet to see anyone ruin their life by doing so. In today's world, your fear of the unknown often prevents you from living your life the way you want to live it. What started as a survival mechanism is now a major reason why some would rather live in misery than risk trying something new and growing their lives.

In life, you not only learn through your own actions, you learn by observing others. You learn how to be afraid in the same way. You can learn to be afraid of a sidelong glance of disapproval because someone else got one. You can learn to be afraid to be yourself because you watched someone else get ridiculed for being who they were. You can also learn to be afraid of losing your job just by hearing horror stories about others who lost theirs. Even if your job is the source of your unhappiness you learn to be afraid to lose it because you allow yourself to feed into the fears of others.

Everyone has that feeling of unease when someone scoffs at what you are wearing. Why? Because that look instantly works on your innate programming that comes out in your insecurities about not fitting in. That insecurity was useful thousands of years ago, when living in a close-net tribe was essential to survival, but today – not so much. Wearing the wrong outfit may hurt your chances of a fast promotion in a law firm or at a publishing group. But is it going to kill you? Is it worth giving up living YOUR own life for?

To be happy, you need to rethink the relationship you have with your fears. Understand that they are not always right. By being mindful of your fears you can greatly reduce the impact they have on your life. You may also be able to use your fears as a sign that you are not where you want to be in life. Your fear of not fitting into a clique at school or work may actually be telling you that it's not the right group of friends or team for you to be with. It might be telling you that it's time to move on.

The next time you are afraid you're going to lose your job, take a moment to think if this is really the job for you. Perhaps you're more creative than anyone else and should be in a different department. Or perhaps you're more of a team player and would work better with a different company. If you feel bad about what you are wearing even though you like your look, look around you. Think about why you are afraid of wearing an outfit. If it's because you want to avoid criticism, perhaps your fear is actually telling you that you're with the wrong group of people – a group that doesn't appreciate YOU for who YOU are.

Once you are able to identify the real reasons behind your fear, you can start to make decisions based on what YOU want, not on what those around you want.

When you freeze and refuse to make a decision, you are actually making a very profound decision. You are deciding to give someone else responsibility for that decision. Either way, you will still have to live with the results. So take responsibility for your fear, and you will take responsibility for your life. More than likely you will find the outcome is far less painful than you originally thought it was. You will also find the results are far better when they are the outcome of your decision to act, rather than giving into your fear.

Exercise – Review Your Social Net

If you've been following along, you have learned to breathe, to meditate and to be mindful of your life. You have see how there is no work/life balance, there is only life. You have also learned how we are, in our hearts and in our basic programming, social creatures.

Let's use this information to take a moment and explore your life through the social networks you have created in the past. Not only can your relationships give you wonderful insight into who you are, they can also show you some interesting insights into some areas of your life that you might want to refresh.

If you were unemployed right now, who would you call and ask if they knew anyone who could help you get a new job? If the answer is no one, it may not be a sign that you're not networking enough. It may be a sign that you need to be working in an entirely different industry. The people who are passionate about their work tend to have a lot of friends in the industries. Not because they're trying to network to the top, but because they love what they do. If you cannot find someone in your industry that you trust enough to help you find a new job, start thinking about who your friends are, what they're doing. It may just be a sign that you need to consider their industries for yourself.

Now it's time to go one step deeper into your friends. Select the people that mean the most in your life. These are the people who make you the happiest or who influence you the most. These are the people you look up to or who you go to when you have a challenge, or whose you simply enjoy being around.

Now write down the similarities each of these people share. This could be based on their geography, their background or education. It could be related to income. Write down those consistencies on a separate page. Now take a third page and write down the character traits that carry across each of those categories.

This is not an exercise to find who you most want to be. Quite the opposite, it is an exercise to find out more about your own Simple Truths, based on those traits you just naturally flock to, often without even realizing it.

Tap into Life's Positive Energy

Have you ever thought about someone and moments later they call you? Have you ever had a bad feeling about a person you just met only to find out later just how right that feeling was? Have you ever watched somebody walk into a room and it just seems to open up to the energy they bring with them? In the West, scientists refer to these types of situations as intuitive responses that work on the subconscious level. In the East, they are attributed to the Universal Energy that each of us is a part of.

Whatever way you are more comfortable describing these events, the reality is, they are very real. They happen to everyone, all the time. If you learn to recognize them you can tap into the energy that exists all around you, and you can find very real opportunities to guide your life in a positive direction. Acknowledging these opportunities can also lead to a broader understanding of the world around you, an expanded awareness of how the universe works, and the ability to join the greater consciousness we all share in.

Most people agree that there is more to the Universe than we are able to sense through sight, smell, sound, touch or taste. But how do you tap into it? How can you benefit from its existence? The answer is you are already tapping into it. You already do benefit from its existence. You just don't realize that you do so every day. By deepening your understanding of the energy that is all around you, you can start to live YOUR life in greater harmony not only with others, but with yourself.

To do this, you must first become aware that it is there. You must then learn to keep open to the energy around you and to recognize the moments when you are truly open to it. By not retreating into your old self and shutting down, you will learn that your needs truly are aligned with the honest needs of those around you. That we do share in a basic human experience, and that you can live in balance with the people and the energy that surrounds all of us.

For now, as with all things, learn to just be aware of the energy that you live in. Acknowledge that it exists so that as you develop and deepen your own consciousness you can began to tap into the energy you encounter.

The Conservation of Energy

Traditional thinking in the West is that the air you breathe is the only thing that surrounds you. That the oxygen that nourishes your body is the only life-giving element you need to be concerned about. But our atmosphere is more like the ocean than the simple mixture of oxygen and nitrogen, carbon dioxide and hydrogen we think of it to be.

We are surrounded by an ocean of energy that never ceases to affect us. Part of this energy can be felt in the air of an approaching thunderstorm. Some of it can be felt when the hairs of your neck rise because you sense something in a dark room. Some of it can be felt when you just get a feeling about someone you just met.

We are surrounded by energy. We are made of energy. It flows around us and through us. It holds our molecules together and creates the world and universe each of us lives in. And yes, it is possible to tap into this energy and connect with others through its channels if you can open yourself up to it.

There is a universal law that Isaac Newton called the "law of conservation of energy". It states that energy can never be created nor destroyed; it can only be converted from one form into another. The sun's energy is turned into food by plants, that food is eaten by us and turned into the energy that keeps us alive. Our bodily wastes, and eventually our bodies, provide energy to the microbes that decompose what is left behind to feed plants and other organisms that exist at various levels. It is more than the cycle of life. It is a pool of life that we all exist in.

The sun's energy that creates life also heats the oceans and the atmosphere. That heat creates the currents that power storms which cool and warm entire continents. It all moves in a circular motion, constantly changing form depending on what the needs of the world are.

Albert Einstein stated way back in the 1920's that everything (including our bodies) is composed of energy. Western scientists are still trying to understand energy, as are Eastern philosophers. Both are getting closer to understanding the fabric of the universe. They are just approaching it from different angles. But they are all coming to the same conclusions – that the energy of life and love is a very real part of our energy of the universe.

It, like all other forms of energy is subject to Newton's Law of Conservation of Energy. It cannot be created nor destroyed, it can only change forms. Like the other laws of the universe, you do not have to understand everything about energy to be bound by its power. But knowing that it exists and understanding it will enable you to better guide your life in harmony with the Universal truths we are all bound to.

You are energy first, and body second.

The Energy You Swim In

When you sit back into a bathtub you don't just get wet. You relax and become one with the water that surrounds you. Your stress melts away as the warmth of the water seeps into your muscles and relaxes you. Your skin softens as the minerals of your bath saturate it. Your mind wanders as your body lets go. Do you know how all of those functions work on the cellular and atomic levels, on the more esoteric levels? Most likely not, yet you do know how to enjoy a bath, right?

The same is true of the energy that you bathe in every day. You don't have to know how it works for it to work. When you step into a soothing tub of water all you have to do is experience it in order to benefit from it. You simply have to let go and allow yourself to enjoy it.

It's no different with the energy around you. You simply have to open up to the fact that you are going to step into the universal tub and let the energy do its work.

Not all that long ago people did not know about the atmosphere that protects us from the sun's radiation. Not long before that, ideas we now take as common knowledge weren't even a consideration. At one point the world was flat, the earth was the center of the universe, and gravity was not even a theory. Today we are still learning about the world and the universe we live in, just at a deeper and more sophisticated level.

Our atmosphere is truly more like the ocean than the simple mixture of gases we credit it with. The atmosphere has currents and tides. It ebbs and flows with the seasons. It carries waves of energy that never stop affecting us. On the physical level this energy can be felt in the air of an approaching thunderstorm. It can be felt in the change of seasons as we orbit around the sun.

It can be felt in the sun as it heats your skin and energizes you with Vitamin D.

On a deeper level the energy we all bathe in is a very real force. In business, people refer to it when they say someone "just gets it." That "it" is a connection someone has with the energy that we all live in. It is that magic moment when you and the energy around you come into alignment and are on the same wavelength, when you are "tapped in."

Whether you recognize it or not, you emanate energy in the same way that you receive energy. You do this without always being aware of it. That is why it is so important that you not only reach out and learn to open up to the positive energy out there, but that you also make sure you only emanate positive energy in return.

When I walk out of my apartment in the morning feeling low and insecure, I find that more people bump into me on the sidewalk. It's as if my circle of energy is small, as if people don't even notice me. On the days that I venture out with my head held high and my shoulders back ready to take on the new day and the world, I find that people open up a path for me to walk down. They physically move out of the way.

The difference is not found in the clothes I wear or the attitude of the other people on the sidewalk. The difference is in the energy I am putting out there.

So enjoy the energy around you. Create the energy you carry with you by simply staying open to it. To recognize it is there will help you create your own whirlpool in which to live. If you can create just a small whirlpool of energy for yourself, you will be surprised at how many people and things will be attracted to you who are able to help you along your way.

You live in your energy every day. It is there for you. It is you. So empower yourself by always bringing in positive energy.

The Power of YES and NO

Tapping into the ocean of energy that is all around you seems like it should be easy. In many ways it is. All you have to do is say yes to it. But to say yes, you have to override your old habits and your old programming. You have to get rid of the old fears and biases that have held you back, to un-peel the old you so that YOU can say yes without hesitation.

Simple Truth

Whine less, breathe more, and smile.

This is more difficult than you might think. The doubts you have, the sarcastic comments you make to yourself, and your return to what you know as safe holds you back from opening up. Those are the security blankets our society has caused you to create. Breaking those old habits is exactly what it takes in order for you to say yes.

Since birth you have been trained to say no. It is a protectionist habit that we all have learned by rote. "No" is the safe path in life. But when you say no, you shut off the flow of energy that can live inside you.

An example I use over and over again is when somebody breaks your heart. When you say "I will love never love again," what do you feel? You feel as if your world has collapsed around you. What happens when that same person comes back to you and says "I am sorry"? Your world opens up and the sun seems to shine brighter doesn't it? It is not just because that other person has opened up to you. It is because you have opened up to them. It is because you have opened yourself up to the energy they are sending you and to the energy that is all around you.

You are completing a circuit. Just like a switch on the wall opens up the current to a light bulb, you can open up your own current by flipping your own switch to the on position.

We have all been in a meeting where somebody brings up an idea for improving business. There is a spark of energy that we all open up to. Until, that is, somebody shoots it down with a remark that has little to do with facts and more to do with fear. Those same people are also usually pretty good about adding a snide comment to ensure the door that just opened gets shut and locked for good.

This is a perfect example of the power that "no" can have. Not only does that person kill the idea, they kill the chance for any other idea to bubble up after it; all because they are more comfortable with the status quo than with the opportunities the future can bring. The second somebody says no, they not only stop the flow of energy, they shut off the opportunities of the universe.

When you follow your old habits, you turn away opportunities for growth and the energy that goes with them. When you act without thinking, without being aware of your actions, you are closing off the opportunities that are out there. I cannot tell you how many wonderful ideas and opportunities were killed with that little word: no. Most of them put away for no other reason than the person uttering those words simply could not open their own heart and mind.

Most of the people I have known that sit on the sidelines of life and say no to other people's ideas, regardless of how good or bad they may be, do so out of their own insecurities, or from their fear of change. They think it is a way to protect themselves; instead it just shows how small they really are if they can fit behind those two letters. If you do not believe in the concept of energy being a living, breathing entity, then sit in a meeting when someone says no.

If you ever find yourself in this situation, then leave. Nothing good will come from an attitude of "no." No problems will ever be solved with the word "no." No progress will ever be made. Because "no" closes every door.

Even worse, it wastes your time.

Train Yourself to Stay Open

The power of NO is exactly why you need to train yourself to stay open. When you feel yourself start to shut down you need to stop yourself. You need to take three deep breaths and think about CaRE. Then you need to consider the alternative to "no" which is "yes."

Yes means realizing that even a bad idea can create great opportunities. I have mentioned Thomas Edison previously. But there are endless stories of repeated failures that led to spectacular success. R. H. Macy failed seven times before his store in New York City finally succeeded. Winston Churchill repeated a grade during elementary school. When he entered Harrow he was placed in the lowest division of the lowest class. Later in life he failed the entrance exam to the Royal Military Academy twice. He was defeated in his first effort to serve in Parliament. He finally became Prime Minister at the age of 62, and later wrote, "Never give in, never give in, never, never, never, never - in nothing, great or small, large or petty - never give in..."

The next time you start to feel yourself closing down, stop. If you feel yourself feeling smaller, stop. Then take three deep breaths and open yourself up by connecting yourself to the world around you. Take a moment to think about whatever is in front of you and start with a short meditation to connect to the world around you.

If there is a bowl or a glass, or even a computer in front of you, use that as a way to meditate on the people who made it. Follow the materials back to their source or think of the people who were behind it. Use the path of energy that helped create whatever is in front of you.

Reacquaint yourself with the fact that everything is connected through energy. Then open yourself up to the good that can come from the positive energy that connects us all. Rely on your network of friends to help you generate positive energy. You will be amazed at how just putting a finger into the pool of energy around you will start to create ripples that will expand and reverberate throughout the world. You will find that a simple meditation on the connectivity of the world will help you see how our energies link us together. Then you will realize how many opportunities could be created as a result of whatever has happened.

If you are experiencing a breakup, find the opportunities you can create from your newfound freedom. Perhaps you can use your time to explore art, music, food or travel. And by doing so, you can open yourself up to meeting new people who will support your passions. If it is a bad business idea, take a moment to follow it and see what can develop out of it. You will be amazed by how many good ideas will spring from a bad one.

The power of positive thinking and positive energy is endless. But you have to stay open before you can tap into it. So use CaRE to train yourself to stay open. Before you continue down your old path, think of how something can be made to work. Be mindful so that you become aware of how quickly you shut down. But take the time to learn how easy it is to remain open.

Tapping into the energy around you truly is like stepping into a bathtub. All the science in the world can try to explain why you will feel wonderful once you are in it. But nothing in the text books will get you to put that first toe into its warmth. You have to do that by yourself.

Compassion & the Spirit of Yes

The Spirit of Yes is based on a very old word and concept. As a concept it can be found in every major religion and is often regarded as one of the highest virtues in each. It is compassion, and from Buddhism to Christianity, Judaism, and Islam, the idea of compassion is revered.

> ***Simple Truth***
>
> *Seek first to understand, and then to be understood.*

It translates to helping others, to being understanding of others, and to have an active desire to alleviate the suffering of others. It is such a powerful concept to the human condition that neuroscientists have studied it for years. They have even located specific points in the brain that relate to compassionate behavior.

If compassion is such a powerful and universal concept, you may ask "where has it been all of my life?" It has been alive and well in Eastern religions and philosophies. It has also been alive and well within you, whether you practice it or not. Compassion has been a part of our programming from day one. It is one of the reasons we can survive in social settings. It is why babies naturally tend to help others rather than just hurt those around them. It has just been hidden by the drive for success and the pursuit of assets that so many people fall into.

Living a Compassionate life and coming back to the Spirit of Yes will keep your channels open. They will help you tap into the energy around you and within you. They will also help you channel that energy in a way that will support YOU on your path.

As you pull back your old layers and clear out the negative programming, work to fill that empty space with compassion.

All you have to do is follow the golden rule and treat others as you want to be treated. Simply help others achieve their Simple Truth, and you will automatically be helping yourself achieve yours. So be a part of the energy surrounding you by opening your heart and saying yes.

While it is important to understand the larger concept of compassion, it is equally important to understand that staying open does not mean you have to say yes to every opportunity that comes by.

If someone asked you to jump off a bridge, you would be a fool to say yes. If someone asked you to steal something for them, you would be just as big a fool. The spirit of yes comes from being accepting, to listening to others, to openly considering what they have to say, to being open to other ideas and ways of life. It also comes from being honest with those around you and to being willing to explore new ideas and new ways to do things. But it does not mean agreeing with everything that comes your way. Simply put, not every request or opportunity supports a compassionate life. Nor will they support your journey or your life.

Being honest means letting people know that your schedule is too busy to take on an additional project for your child's school. It means being honest and telling a client that you cannot deliver a project just because they asked for it on their desk in the morning. It means letting someone know why an idea is a bad one, but then giving them the opportunity to suggest alternatives. It means that even if something is not the right opportunity for you, you will take the time to suggest some ways in which it can be.

Living a compassionate life in today's world often requires a little more work, but it keeps the doors open and the energy flowing. It also implies that progress can be made if the people involved work together to overcome whatever obstacle is in the path to success. It reminds people that change is coming, which can be a very scary prospect to a lot of people, and lets them know that stagnation is not an option.

If someone asks you to bake cookies for a school event and you simply do not have the time to bake then say just that. Say, "I would love to help out, but I simply don't have any time this week. Is there something else I can do?"

By telling the truth and leaving the door open, you are not stopping the flow of energy. You are maintaining your life so that you don't trap yourself into pursuing someone else's needs at the cost of your own. At the same time you are keeping the door open to new ideas of how you can help.

When you start living in the Spirit of Yes you will find that it acts as a self-filtering system. More opportunities will start to come to you that are in line with your own needs. They will start to match your priorities and YOUR life.

The same can be true in a business environment. If you find yourself instinctively thinking why an idea will not work, stop and ask how could you make it work? Ask yourself, if not this, how else could it be done?

By saying "no," all you are doing is killing the momentum of all ideas that could be created in the future. You are also killing the momentum of progress. By saying "yes" you are not necessarily committing to moving an idea forward, but you are saying "let's explore this direction."

Remember, you can always say "no" at any point in the future. But once you have said "no" the door is closed forever. And then you really will have no options but to keep shutting down.

So keep the door open to new ideas, new ways of doing things, and new opportunities. You will find it perpetuates itself over and over.

The Wisdom of Caution

The Spirit of Yes is a very powerful concept. But it must be tempered with the Wisdom of Caution. People will always approach you with ideas that go against compassion. It is up to you to see them for what they are, and to turn away.

We have all felt it. You smile as you are introduced and for some reason you just don't feel right about the person in front of you. Perhaps they seem "creepy" or "slimy." So you become cautious. And you should.

Have you ever walked down a street and had a feeling that this was the wrong street to walk down? Have you ever gotten a bad feeling about a person? You are not quite sure why, you hardly know them, but you just know there is something not good. It is not fear that you feel, but caution.

It comes from the small cues you see in the way someone acts. It comes from the energy they put out. When this happens to you, stop yourself from shutting down and closing yourself off. Instead remain open to meeting the person before you. Smile and commit to giving them a chance, but also remain aware of their energy and the signals you may feel.

Remember, bad decisions do not happen on their own; they are the result of a series of bad choices that put you in the position of having to make a bad decision. So make the decision to meet new people and try new things. But also make your choices with an awareness of the energy around you. Free yourself up to sense what is going on behind the words someone says, and always leave yourself an option to walk away if you must.

Simple Truth

You are not what you do. You are how you do it.

The sensation of warning that comes when something is not right is one that you want to listen to. It is a voice that your brain uses when it senses that something about your current circumstances is similar to situations you may have been in before. It is your brain trying to tell you that what is happening now is going down the wrong path. In effect it is your brain saying "I don't have the time to tell you everything that I am seeing, but from everything you have experienced in all of the years of your life, and from the energy I am sensing right now, you are getting yourself into a bad situation. Turn back now." It is why you have "gut feelings" about something. You can't explain why something is good or bad, but you just know it is.

Perhaps you have just seen a man from across a party, and you just have to meet him. He is attractive, he is well dressed and seems to have everything you thing you want. But when you meet him, something just doesn't feel right. Perhaps it is the way he looks at you, or takes a sharp tone to his voice. This is your heart telling you that this person's energy is wrong. Even if your brain may be telling you "this is someone you should meet." Your heart and instinct are saying walk away.

Listen to them. They are picking up on that person's or that alley's energies even if you can't see them. They are more real and relevant than all the images you see through your eyes. And yes, you can do so in the Spirit of Yes.

"I would love to, but it is getting late so why don't we meet for coffee this week?"

"Thank you but I'm walking home with friends. But can I call you?"

All of these responses are in the Spirit of Yes. They just slow down the events that are underway so that you can take a few moments to think and stay on YOUR path.

Assert Your Positive Self

Have you ever met someone who just seems electric? They have an energy around them that seems to welcome you in, and everyone just naturally wants to be around them. They are real, they are genuine. There is no façade that makes you constantly question what their real intent is. When they walk in, it is as if a tidal wave of love and positive energy just entered the room; and in a lot of ways, it has.

Just as you can pick up on the energy that is out there you also emanate it. Even if you can't explain why you get a feeling about someone, you still get those instinctive feelings in a very real way. We all do. Which is why it's so important to ensure your emotions and energies are positive ones.

You may think you can fool people with a look, but people are more transparent than we think. People pick up on the nuances and the energy you put out there. They see through the little poses you throw up. Especially once people start to know you.

It may be as simple as the way you smile when you are upset that tells people that behind your smile you don't really want to do something that you are agreeing to. Perhaps it is the way you answer too quickly and then find yourself trapped defending a position you don't even believe in. So before you find yourself in a position you do not want to be in, slow down your actions. Take a moment to think about what you are doing before you respond. If you feel pressured to respond, take a moment. Use CaRE to make sure that your responses are in line with your true self.

Taking your time is one of the best ways to assert your positive self. By saying "just a moment" you can make sure of your actions before you act. You can make sure you know why you are doing something so that your reasoning makes sense. More important, you make sure you are genuine in your actions and truly behind your actions, not blindly moving forward based on someone else's beliefs.

Asserting yourself in a positive way keeps the door open. It also makes sure that the open door is the right one for you to walk through. It all comes down to how you communicate yourself in words, in action, and in energy.

Create Your Own Vortex

We all know a true believer, that person who charges forward with such a conviction that it seems as if nothing can stop them. They are the ones who refuse to waver or cave into the notion that it can't be done. It can be for something as simple as going camping one weekend, and not wavering even when the weather report turns sour. It can be as powerful as a candidate who stands up for what they believe in, whether it is a popular choice or not. It does not always end up in the right direction, but that conviction can move mountains.

No matter the outcome, the funny thing about a true believer is that people will get in line and follow them anywhere. People will join a crusade they want to believe in. They will also drop out of a crusade just as quickly if the faith in the cause wavers.

The lesson in this is if you don't believe in your own path, nobody else will. If on the other hand you pursue your dream with undying faith, people will take notice and get in line to support you. Rarely will someone help if you do not take the first step. Even more rarely will people continue to support your dream if you don't support it yourself.

So if you have found something you believe in and are passionate about it put it out there. Some people will laugh. Others will follow. Don't worry about the ones that laugh. They were laughing before you ever offered an open door to them. It is their way of saying "no, I'm afraid of thinking something new." But those that follow, those that support you, are the ones who will be there for you no matter what. They are the ones you want walking with you along your path. But that is never going to happen unless you take the first step and put your dream out there.

Creating your own vortex is like a creating a whirlpool. Once you start it people and opportunities start to take notice of what you are doing. They start to get pulled in to your ideas and your energy. They start to tell their friends about what you are doing and those friends start to support you also.

Have you ever wondered how a film gets made? It starts with someone who has an idea that they are passionate about. They start to tell other people about their idea. Soon enough a talented star or a name director hears about it from someone else who has heard about it. They ask to be a part of the idea. People start to notice. Someone with money comes along and says "I like this idea, especially with the talent you have attached to it. I'm willing to invest if you have a way to distribute it." Someone else comes along and says "now that you have the money and talent for your film, I have a chain of theaters you can show it in." Soon enough you have the talent you need, the money you need, and you have the theaters you need. You have a film.

Simple Truth

Look outside your heart to dream.
Look inside your heart to awaken.

Of course none of that happens overnight. But the difference between having an idea and having a film starts with just one person who is determined to make their idea real. They create a vortex that attracts more and more people until they have an entire production behind them.

The same is true of any endeavor. Just putting your idea out there does not guarantee it will be a success. But if you do not put it out there, it will never even have a chance to grow. It all starts by creating your own vortex. By putting your idea out there and nurturing it with the right energy.

No matter what your goal is, start with the first step. When you rise in the morning, take a moment to think about what you are going to achieve that day. If you are looking for a new job, say it. Vocally say it and write it down. It does not guarantee someone will call you with a job offer, but you will be surprised at how just sending it out into the energy that exists around all of us you can start your own vortex. Start talking to people about the type of job you're looking for. Just remember nothing happens overnight. Everything takes time. So start early. Put your energy out there. Start talking to people about your idea. Start your own buzz and your own vortex. You will be surprised at what can happen.

On a smaller scale, but just as important, start creating a little vortex every time you wake up or go out. When you wake up in the morning, take a moment to align yourself with the world you're waking up to. Ask yourself what you're going to do that day. If you are going out with friends for the evening, ask yourself who you are. Are you confident? Are you funny? Are you in a good mood or a bad one?

Make sure you believe in whatever you are saying or doing. Be true to who you are and what you are doing. Be in the moment and believe in the good choices that you are making. People will notice the difference. The positive people that you want around you will join you and defend you even if you are proposing something they may not initially want to do.

Live Your Karma

Karma does exist. It is part of the energy that surrounds each of us. Only the payback does not wait until the afterlife or even the next life. It happens in the here and now. Everything you do adds a layer onto the core of who you are. Every action you take has a consequence that affects your energy on the inside and on the outside, for better and for worse.

Karma is not just relegated to the larger decisions in your life. It applies to everything you do. It comes alive when you feel guilty about some slight you made when you were a child even though it may have been negligible. It shows itself when you just can't shrug off that smug comment you made the other night.

Karma is not about large acts or small acts. It is about the energy you put out into the world and the universe. It can bubble up inside you and come out as guilt. It can come back from business associates who no longer trust you and who are no longer willing to go out on a limb like they used to. It can be even larger as doors begin to close in front of you and your opportunities seem to shrink before they even present themselves. And yes, it can manifest itself in even bigger ways.

When you were young you had no idea how your comments affected others. You never realized how cruel your small jests could be to someone who was sensitive. Yet you still feel some of them now. Don't worry. You cannot go back and repair everything you did. Nobody can. And that is not how you change your karma. You change it by playing it forward. Now that you understand how your actions can have a ripple effect, you can stop doing them. Now is the time to rethink and start acting differently. Now is the time to start acting compassionately.

Stop making the small asides you may do so naturally. Stop making the comments that make you feel better and make someone else feel worse. If you find yourself saying "just kidding," in order to reduce the sting of what you just said, stop giving yourself a reason to have to say it. Some people try to assert control over their world by tearing others down. It makes them think they are in control. In reality it is just an attempt to cover up their own insecurities. The downside is all of those little comments will start to come back to bite them as they erode the very world they were trying to protect.

So if you will not think of someone else's feelings. Think of your own karma. Get in the habit of watching the energy you put out. Also become aware of the opportunities that come into your world when you treat the world and yourself well.

Every Action

In 1687 Sir Isaac Newton compiled three physical laws that describe the relationship between forces of nature and a physical body. They are appropriately called Newton's Laws. They have been expressed in various ways over the centuries, but the most important states: To every action there is always an equal and opposite reaction. This is not only true for physical objects, but also for metaphysical objects also.

As you grow and evolve, as you assert yourself, you will find that others will push back against your efforts to grow. As you start to break free of your old patterns to follow your Simple Truth, some of the people you know will start to feel uncomfortable about what they see as change; and change is scary for a lot of people.

Not only will it make them realize that their world is changing, it will make them realize that they are not. They will want you to return to the person they knew you to be. They will do most anything to ensure that their world will remain the same, even though that is impossible.

Be aware of this as you begin to follow your Simple Truth. It is not enough to simply kick down the walls you have created around you. That is the easy way, but kicking down the walls around you can cause your house to collapse.

You need to be compassionate to those around you. You need to be sensitive to your surroundings and to the people who care about you; because they do care, whether you believe it right now or not.

A sudden change at your office is an action that can elicit an equal and opposite reaction from your employers, which could end your employment. Demanding your friends and associates accept the "new you" is an action that can cause people to recoil and turn away.

Evolution takes time. It has taken 40,000 years to get to this point in human evolution. So take your time to talk with those around you. Help them understand the YOU behind the you they know.

A rapid release of energy causes violent destruction as witnessed in volcanoes, earthquakes and tidal waves. The slow process of tides and waves create beautiful beaches and barrier reefs. The slow release of energy from the sun creates life on earth, while the rapid release through solar flares causes disruption.

Change is inevitable. It is the only constant in life. So take your time. Enjoy being a witness to your own evolution. Just make sure those around you can enjoy your rebirth as much as you.

Constantly Evolve Your Simple Truth

Finding and living your own Simple Truth should not stop when you close this book. It should be part of your never-ending exploration of life and a never-ending part of your own personal evolution. Constantly challenge yourself, constantly seek out new knowledge and ways to do things, and constantly seek out information, ideas and people. The world is an ever changing place that will continually amaze and surprise you. So enjoy the process of change and live YOUR life.

Challenge Your Automatic Pilot

It is possible to quickly learn just how fully you operate on automatic pilot. You can also challenge it and shut it off just as quickly. Your programming creates your habits. The very things you do by rote are to most likely to be based on your old programming. So by challenging your habits you can start to reprogram your behavior.

I constantly ask people to challenge themselves in simple ways. If you normally follow one route to go to the store or the office try changing it. See how uncomfortable you become or how quickly you try to talk yourself out of deviating from your normal path. You might find your inner voice kicking in with comments like "this is ridiculous, the other way is shorter," or "I already have a route down." If you order the same thing at lunch every day, why not change and try something new?

What is the worst that can happen if you order something new or drive a new route? You do not like what you eat? You take another ten minutes getting somewhere? Is that really so bad? In today's risk-averse world, deviating from your staid course is easy and the downside is usually pretty small in comparison to the ability to live your own life, freely and openly. It might even make you chuckle or outright laugh when you begin to realize how uncomfortable you become simply by challenging the accepted way you do things. You might also be surprised at all the new and wonderful things you start to experience just by making some small changes in how you life.

Covet Your Time

Take out your tape measure again. See how many inches you have left. No matter how far you stretch it, your time is limited on this earth. So be careful of it. Protect it. Cherish it. Most important enjoy it. It is the one commodity you cannot save, you cannot lock away, and you can never get back. If you do not spend it, it will be lost forever before you know it. So be aware of how you spend your time.

Take the time to do good things. Take the time to give to others. Make sure you spend your time wisely. Most important, don't be afraid to be selfish with your time. Make sure that when you give it to someone else, you give it out sparingly. Look at your time as an investment and dole it out as carefully as you would money. Make sure that you spread it evenly and diversify how you spend your time. It is the best way to garner a positive return on everything that you do. But also make sure you keep some for yourself. That in itself is often the best way to invest your most precious commodity.

Control Your Mobile

I was meeting an old friend whom I had not seen in quite some time. We were in the middle of a great conversation when his mobile rang. He looked at me apologetically and said "I'm sorry, but it's my cell." He talked for a minute or so to whoever it was, then he spent the rest of lunch apologizing for taking the call.

He laughed when I said, "the amazing thing about mobile phones is they have a silence switch that means you do not have to answer them. You also have an answering service that will take messages for you." He said he knew, but he also felt compelled to answer, as if the person on the other side of the call would be devastated if he were out of touch for even a minute. His jaw literally dropped for a second when I said "how much is your cell phone paying you for that service?" Then he nodded and understood.

The question is do you own your mobile phone? Or does it own you? You live in a very plugged in world with 24/7 access to almost every kind of device imaginable. Every one of those devices was created to help you. They were designed to be a convenience, to make your life easier. That is why every device has a mute button and an off button. That is why you also have to take an action to actually connect a call. That also means you can also choose to NOT take an action and to NOT connect a call.

Do not let the devices you possess rule your life. Leave them at home from time to time. Turn them off on a Sunday. Choose not to answer a call. It can be amazing to see what happens to your life when you take control of your devices. A day can actually be a time when you just enjoy the day itself.

Enjoy Electronic Free Weekends

It almost sounds ridiculous to write this. But, I have an electronic free weekend once a month. Once a month! Just reading my own words makes it sound like I am addicted to my email and voicemail and whatever social networks can be dreamed up. It sounds like I should be doing this every weekend. After all, it is my life.

But then I realized two things. First, I enjoy contacting and keeping up with people through email and texts and Twitter and Facebook. Second, I also realized leaving that alone for a weekend every month reminds me that these systems were designed to be used by me, when I want to use them. They were not designed to compel me to constantly be on call.

So yes, once a month I log off and shut down for a weekend. It allows my mind to process all of the ideas that I did not have time to process during the week. It's worth trying. Or you might try just reducing your time online over the weekends or during the week. By stopping yourself at that point where you are no longer seeking to interact or find new information, but are just surfing, you give your mind a chance to process all of those creative thoughts and ideas that you may miss.

By giving your conscious mind a rest, you allow your subconscious thoughts to become active and began to influence the rest of your life. You might be amazed at what comes up, or how much extra sleep you find yourself getting.

Dry, Dry, Drink

A dear, dear friend of mine named Bruce Weldyn came up with a concept he calls Dry, Dry, Drink. It stuck with me the first moment I heard it, and I have passed it on to many, many more. It is so simple, yet so life-changing that I cannot rate it too highly. Nor can I rate him too highly as a compassionate human and a brilliant thinker.

Life cannot be all work and no play. After all, we are on this planet so that we can grow as human beings and as souls, spirits, beings of energy or whatever else you want to call us. We are here to explore and experience all that life has to offer so that we can evolve.

Yes, we are here to enjoy our lives, but we can only grow if we do so in a responsible manner. Only then, can we find the harmony and balance we are looking for. And the concept of Dry, Dry, Drink is a wonderful way to find that harmony between life's pleasures and life's responsibilities.

Like me, Bruce does not feel that drinking is a sin in and of itself. A moderate amount of drink from time to time is a wonderful way to relieve stress and let the creative muses run a bit. At the same time, there can be tremendous issues in going too far with anything; hence the rationale of Dry, Dry, Drink.

It simply translates to moderation. If you have a drink one day, then go without for the next two days. Alternatively if you go without a drink for two days, it is okay to have a drink on the third. If you have a drink two nights in a row, then go for the next four days without. If you cannot moderate yourself like this, if you cannot go for two days without a drink, then you may have a problem.

It does not just go for drinking either. We can do almost anything to an obsessive level, and it hits a point where it can become unhealthy. So remember to take some time off from whatever you are doing. Look at the ways you release the pressures of today's world. Incorporate meditation into your life and take the time for reflection. It will give you time to think and ponder what direction you want to take, rather than just running full speed ahead.

Apply the concept of Dry, Dry, Drink to all aspects of your life, in order to truly find balance.

Most People Are Pretty Nice

When I was young I asked my older brother if people were inherently good or evil. He thought about it for a while before answering. Finally he said, "the reason every car window is not smashed after being parked on the street all night, and the reason every antenna is not bent or torn out is that the vast majority of people don't want to hurt someone else's property. The only reason cities are not in a case of constant riot is that people actually want to live in peace if they are given the chance."

Peace and compassion are the most natural state for people. We desire company and friendship. We desire love. Yes, there will always be a small minority who use violence as a release or to get what they want. But for the most part, most people play fairly. Most people are honest. Most people are loving.

So expect the best. But be prepared for the worst. Give people a chance to be good. Approach them with compassion but watch for their response. You will most likely be surprised at how willing people are to help. Just be prepared if the alternative happens.

Leave yourself a path to walk away from that small percent that is not.

Ask is Not a Four Letter Word

The only way to get what you want out of life is to ask for it. There is nothing wrong with asking people for their insights, for their assistance, or for their help. That simple act is the largest part of creating a safety net of people who are willing to help each other. That is part of the give and take in life. Make sure you help others, but don't be afraid to ask for help when you need it.

It's not always the easiest thing to put yourself out there and admit you need help. It goes against our nature. It puts us in a position of weakness. The thought of rejection undermines the opportunity for growth. Overcome this, and a world of help will open up to you. Be polite, be humble and be honest when you do it. But do it.

Also don't be afraid or embarrassed to go further and ask the energy that surrounds and flows through everyone and everything for your happiness. You might be surprised at how willing people are to reach out and give you the help, the comfort and the love you need. You might also be surprised at how the energy of the world responds to your needs.

Just don't forget to give back as much as you can. Love and energy are doors that swing open and closed. So keep yours open by returning more than you ask for.

Ask Questions, Make No Judgments

To get answers you need to ask questions. It is the way we learn and grow. Just be fair to yourself when you look for answers. It is far too easy to beat yourself up if the answers you're seeking aren't the ones you ended up with. That is part of the learning process. No matter what the answer happens to be they will help you learn and evolve.

So be sure to ask questions, but beware of passing judgment when you do, especially on your own actions. Frame your questions positively. Instead of asking yourself why you did something that was wrong. Ask yourself what could have been a better way to handle a situation. Most important, don't forget to congratulate yourself when you do something right. It's far too easy to berate ourselves and wallow in the mud, than to pick ourselves up with a few little comments.

When you hear your inner voice point out an issue, or nitpick your actions to death, stop and ask yourself, "What are you trying to discover with this question?" Be honest with yourself. If you are just being judgmental, then stop. If your line of questioning is not going to lead you to self discovery, then it is not coming from a positive place.

So ask, but keep it positive.

Do Not Forget To Love

One of my favorite lines from a movie comes from the first few minutes of a wonderful little film called Love Actually. It's narrated by Hugh Grant:

> "Whenever I get gloomy with the state of the world, I think about the arrivals gate at Heathrow Airport. General opinion's starting to make out that we live in a world of hatred and greed, but I don't see that. It seems to me that love is everywhere. Often it's not particularly dignified or newsworthy, but it's always there – fathers and sons, mothers and daughters, husbands and wives, boyfriends, girlfriends, old friends. When the planes hit the Twin Towers, as far as I know none of the phone calls from the people on board were messages of hate or revenge – they were all messages of love. If you look for it, I've got a sneaky feeling you'll find that love actually is all around."

Love is one of the most crucial ingredients to being human. And life without love is rarely what anyone would call a good life. However, love is not about giving yourself away. It is about being true to YOURSELF and finding a partner who helps you be YOU.

Do not squander your own well being and emotion on someone who is not there for YOU. Take the time to find someone who augments and supports the real YOU. Yes, it is wonderful to have friends and supporters. But love? Search for the ONE who is for YOU.

Commit 100%

Most people relate success to shows of wealth and status. It is almost as if the word itself is tainted. As if you have to sell out in some way in order to succeed. But that is not what success means at all. It has nothing to do with wealth. It has to do with achieving your goals, with living your own Simple Truth.

Yes, for some it is only measured by how much money they have. For others it is simply being content in everything that they do. No matter what your goal is, achieving it will not bring you happiness. But working toward it will. You can never find ultimate spiritual enlightenment. But you can walk the path toward it for all eternity. And enjoy every step of the way.

Success is not the same for everyone. But having a goal will give you a path to follow. Walking on your path, no matter where it leads, will give you contentment and happiness. It will give you knowledge and help to fulfill your needs. So no matter what your goal is, make sure it is YOUR goal.

Also make sure you commit to it fully, but do not over-commit. I know some people say give it 110%, but that is an easy way to lose your way and find that you are simply giving more than you have for the long-term. Commit what you have, but don't lose YOURSELF while you do it.

Do your best to achieve your goals and commit to being the best at whatever it is that you are doing. If your goal is to become a yogi, then commit to it and work to become the best yogi you can be. If your goal is to be an artist, then strive to learn the techniques you need to know. Learn how to work with a brush, pen and ink, or clay, so that you can express yourself through your art. If your goal is to become an accountant, then commit to being the best accountant you can be. But never lose yourself so deeply that you forget who YOU are.

You can be true to yourself and also true to your craft, no matter what your craft is. And that balanced commitment is what will bring you happiness every day you wake up.

Everything Is Not What You Want

The easy way out in life is to say "I want it all." It gives you a free pass to underachieve on everything. Because you can always say, "hey I reached for the stars and fell short." Why ask for something knowing you will never achieve it. Especially when that is not what you really want.

People who say they want everything actually know very little about themselves. They have not taken the time to find out who they are and what they want. So remember, the next time somebody asks what you want. Tell them. After all, everything is not really what you want. What you really want is more specific. What you want is happiness. So why not go for it?

Tell everyone you simply want to be happy. Then commit to it.

What Will You Give Up

A friend asked me not too long ago what it would take for him to become an award winning director. I thought about it and said, "The question is not what it would take to achieve it, but what are you willing to give up?"

As I have said before. There is a natural amount of talent that goes into being the best at anything. Anyone can become a surgeon or an artist. Anyone can become an athlete. But to be the best means sacrificing. It means giving up something for your dream. Becoming the best often means giving up a traditional family life. It may mean giving up a part of your personal life or certain friendships.

Getting a million dollars is not the hardest thing to do in the world. Not losing yourself along the way is.

Look at all the celebrities who did whatever it took to get their name in lights. Now look at what they had to do to get there and how they lived once they did. The next time you ask yourself what you want. Stop to ask yourself what you are willing to give up in order to get it.

You will probably find that the costs rarely justify the gold. So really think about what YOU want. Make sure it is something that supports your own Simple Truths. Then go after it with everything you have. Only then will you find true happiness.

Simple Truth

Always begin with the end in mind.

12365828R00155

Made in the USA
Charleston, SC
30 April 2012